Speech & Equality

■
Speech & Equality
Do We Really Have to Choose?

Edited by
Gara LaMarche
Foreword by
Norman Dorsen

New York University Press
New York and London

New York University Press
New York and London

Copyright © 1996 by New York University Press
All rights reserved

Library of Congress Cataloging-in-Publication Data
Speech and equality : do we really have to choose? / edited by Gara LaMarche : foreword by Norman Dorsen.
p.   cm.
ISBN 0-8147-5091-5 (cloth : alk. paper).—ISBN 0-8147-5105-9 (pbk. : alk. paper)
1. Freedom of speech—United States. 2. Abortion services—Law and legislation—United States. 3. Hate speech—United States. 4. Sexual harrassment—Law and legislation—United States.
I. LaMarche, Gara.
KF4772.S64   1996   96-4482
342.73'0853—dc20   CIP
[347.302853]

New York University Press books are printed on acid-free paper, and their binding materials are chosen for strength and durability.

10 9 8 7 6 5 4 3 2 1

Contents

Acknowledgments	vii
Foreword by Norman Dorsen	ix
Introduction by Gara LaMarche	1

One. Abortion Clinic Protests

David Cole	9
Sylvia Law	21
Catherine Albisa	26
Discussion	37

Two. Hate Crimes/Hate Speech

Ira Glasser	55
Martin Redish	64
Randall Kennedy	70
Discussion	72

Three. Workplace Harassment

Susan Deller Ross	101
Deborah Ellis	122
Wendy Kaminer	130
Discussion	135
Notes	151
Contributors	163

Acknowledgments

Thanks to Roland Algrant, Norman Dorsen, Ira Glasser, Sylvia Law, Steve Shapiro, and Nadine Strossen, who helped shape my idea for the gathering of civil rights and civil liberties thinkers that led to this book; Christina Derry, whose assistance was invaluable in the book's early stages; and all my friends and colleagues at the American Civil Liberties Union and Human Rights Watch, my organizational homes. I hope this book does justice to their tradition of robust debate among people who share basic values.

Foreword by Norman Dorsen

Conflict is the essence of civil liberty because individual or group rights are rarely, if ever, bestowed willingly. From the day King John was forced at Runnymede to recognize that his barons had certain prerogatives, to the present era, when racial minorities, women, and homosexuals fight for a place at the table, and others seek to defend such precious rights as free expression, due process, and religious liberty, the din of political, judicial, and sometimes violent battle can be heard.

In the United States, the courts are a principal forum for resolving conflicts because of their power, under our system of law, to determine what the Constitution means. In most lawsuits where rights are claimed the antagonists are an assertive individual and a resistant government. But on closer inspection the government is often acting as a surrogate for private interests not usually represented in the courtroom. For example, whoever the parties might be in a particular case, abortion litigation is at bottom a face-off between colliding interests asserted on behalf of a pregnant woman and her fetus or unborn child.

Racial cases are also illustrative. When slaves petitioned for freedom in the nineteenth century, they were countered by the assertion of property rights by slaveholders. More recently, in *Brown v. Board of Education*, which voided intentionally segregated public schools, the contentions of the African-American plaintiffs based on equal protection of the laws were disputed by arguments for freedom of association presented on behalf of white parents and students. And the more recent constitutional struggle over the validity of affirmative action programs in education and employment for nonwhites and women has turned on contrasting visions of the meaning of equality in the Fourteenth Amendment as championed by the respective parties.

It is against this background that the Arthur Garfield Hays Civil Liberties Program of New York University School of Law and the Free Expression Project of Human Rights Watch brought together the scholars presented in this volume to discuss three highly topical issues in which, at least on the surface, conflicts exist between rights of free expression and rights of equality or privacy—laws that restrict protests at abortion clinics, criminalize "hate speech" and pornography, and regulate verbal harassment based on race or sex in the workplace.

These conflicts present sharply controverted constitutional claims that require resolution in courts and in public opinion, and if civil libertarians are to perform their usual advocacy role, they must sort out the issues and decide where to place their weight. Of course, if one is indifferent to the constitutional principle on one side of any of these conflicts, the contest evaporates and the other side prevails by default. But the impressive scholars, lawyers, and activists represented in this volume do not take this easy path. Without exception, they appreciate the importance of the values supporting free speech as well as those supporting equality and privacy, so that when they favor one or the other constitutional interest it is only after carefully weighing the opposing interest.

Indeed, their central purpose is not to declare winners and losers, but rather to clarify for lawyers and lay persons, both liberal and conservative, the nature of the tensions between the constitutional provisions. In this spirit, several writers maintain that the Constitution is not a zero-sum game, and that superficial conflicts between free speech and equality or privacy principles often can be resolved through imaginative and sympathetic analysis.

The issues discussed in this book are at the top of the national agenda. New controversies arise almost monthly, highlighted by the fanatical murders of physicians working at abortion clinics. Similarly, new prosecutions are being brought for hate speech, and there is a steady stream of cases on workplace harassment and censorship of sexually explicit films and other art forms. In view of all this activity, what the contributors to this book say will have immediate relevance to the ongoing public debate. Policymakers and private citizens alike would do well to read and digest their views.

Introduction by Gara LaMarche

While the constitutional dilemmas discussed in this book are perennial ones, there could hardly be a better time than now to air them. All around us are voices asking whether our deep-seated national attachment to freedom of expression serves to cover—and even stimulate—discrimination and violence. In the ashes of Oklahoma City, some see sparks set off by incendiary talk-show hosts. In the blood of slain doctors and abortion clinic staff from Brookline, Massachusetts, to Pensacola, Florida, some see the footprints of those who picket women's health centers carrying graphic signs and shouting angry words at their patrons. In light of these events, we urgently need to examine the apparent conflicts between two important and cherished values—speech and equality—and to survey the line between protected speech and illegal acts.

While the discussion is timely, the debate is virtually timeless. It is also peculiarly American. In the 1930s, defending the American Civil Liberties Union (ACLU) against criticisms by the *Nation* magazine and others for representing the free speech rights of domestic fascists, ACLU General Counsel Arthur Garfield Hays called himself a "free speech absolutist," a claim that has echoed down through the years in controversies ranging from Nazi marches to pornography on the Internet. But what does it mean to be an absolutist today? Did Hays misplace his faith that racism, sexism, and repressive ideologies would fail in the marketplace of ideas?

From its earliest days, the American Civil Liberties Union, the leading free speech organization in the country, has also been a strong advocate for equality, from its campaign for a federal antilynching law in the 1920s to its involvement in *Shelley v. Kramer, Brown v. Board of Education,* and other cases in the 1940s and the 1950s, to its present-day and often pioneering work, on voting rights and educational equity.

Yet today, feminist scholar Catherine MacKinnon claims, to what often seems a rising chorus of approval, that the law of equality and the law of freedom of speech are on a collision course in this country. I hope she's wrong. Indeed, Norman Dorsen and I conceived the "Speech vs. Equality" symposium that gave rise to this book because we believe MacKinnon's premise must be carefully examined against the hard facts of particular controversies that have divided the civil rights and civil liberties communities. For that reason, Human Rights Watch and New York University School of Law's Arthur Garfield Hays Program assembled a thoughtful and diverse group of writers, scholars, and thinkers in an attempt to explore and illuminate these issues. This book is the result of those efforts. It is divided into three parts, each relating to a particular clash between free speech and equality values.

During the civil rights and antiwar movements of the 1960s, no one seriously asserted that protest tactics such as the occupation of university presidents' offices or vandalism at military facilities, was protected by the First Amendment. It was viewed as civil disobedience. Is there any reason to think differently about blockades and other disruptive activities that take place against abortion clinics? What about the noise and distance regulations enacted in response to these tactics? David Cole, a Georgetown University law professor, asks some troubling questions about whether the aggressive stance of pro-choice advocates in going after Operation Rescue confers upon the group a visibility, and a martyrdom, it doesn't merit. New York University Professor Sylvia Law thinks pro-choice advocates may be *too* solicitous of the rights of antichoice demonstrators and would create a larger "bubble of privacy" around clinics. Catherine Albisa, a reproductive rights attorney, believes the conflict has been exaggerated—that clinic personnel are primarily concerned about violence, not speech.

No one argues any longer that free speech or association principles come into play when a tavern owner posts a sign that says she refuses to serve blacks. But is thought being punished when a criminal assault is subject to a greater penalty because the victim was chosen on the basis of his or her race? If not, how can such an attempt be demonstrated without a wide-ranging inquiry into the beliefs, motivations, and associations of the accused? Ira Glasser, executive director of the American Civil Liberties Union, sets forth a strong case against campus "hate speech codes," but thinks that such enhanced penalties for violent acts may pass First Amendment muster. Northwestern University Law Professor Martin Redish believes such laws punish motivation, and that the principle behind them could have been used to prosecute draft-card burners. Harvard University Law Professor Randall Kennedy, in a spirited exchange with Glasser, takes a different tack: he believes the ACLU's alliance with Rep. Henry Hyde on a bill to bar private campus speech codes tramples on the academic freedom of the institutions involved.

Everyone agrees that the First Amendment does not protect a supervisor's verbal suggestion that an employee go to bed with him in order to obtain a promotion. But is free expression trampled if an employer can be penalized for maintaining a sexist or a racist working atmosphere, even if no individualized harassment takes place? Can posters, T-shirts, and photographs be considered in making such a determination? And if so, where should the lines be drawn? Or, as Justice Ruth Bader Ginsburg, another former ACLU general counsel, put it in her questions during oral arguments in the *Harris v. Forklift* sexual harassment case, "Is it as simple as saying that if one sex has to put up with something the other doesn't, that's sexual harassment?" Susan Deller Ross, director of Georgetown University Law Center's Sex Discrimination Clinic, is inclined to see it this way, and she wonders why those concerned with workers' free speech rights focus on this of all issues. Wendy Kaminer, who writes on social policy issues, worries that the policing of workers' and employers' comments and posters sometimes has more to do with political correctness than sex discrimination. Deborah Ellis, legal director of the NOW Legal Defense and Education Fund, argues for more emphasis on the special nature of the workplace—not a traditional forum, like a university, for the robust exchange of ideas.

In my own efforts to figure out how to answer these questions as a member of the Human Rights Watch staff, as well as an ACLU board member and chair of its free speech committee, I found myself in the position of having to defend my First Amendment bona fides to my colleagues when I took the position that the Constitution is not violated by carefully drawn sentencing regulations enhancing the penalty for a person who attacks someone because of his or her race. Or when I voted with the majority of the ACLU board that images and speech can be an element of sexual harassment when they create a working atmosphere that makes it difficult, if not impossible, for a woman to work at a job.

Among many people who share common values of respect for civil rights and civil liberties, these challenges have produced genuine confusion and division about how to strike a balance between apparently competing values, and whether indeed a balance should be struck. Is the Constitution a zero-sum game, or can these situations be handled in a way that does justice to both free speech and equality principles?

Of one thing I'm certain: Henry Louis Gates, Jr., had it right when he wrote that the strongest argument for regulating speech is the unreflective nature of most of the arguments for the other side—the tendency of those "who invoke the First Amendment mantra . . . to fall into a trance, oblivious to further argument and evidence." The scholars and advocates assembled in this book came together to break that "trance." The essays and discussions in this collection are the result of this effort.

■ PART ONE

Abortion Clinic Protests

■ David Cole

It is often said that the First Amendment demands protection not for the speech we love, but for the speech we hate. But the history of First Amendment jurisprudence suggests that it often works otherwise. For example, many of the most speech-protective First Amendment decisions were issued during the civil rights era, when the federal courts were allied with the civil rights movement against Southern state and local officials.[1] In this period, the Supreme Court placed the protection of the First Amendment behind the voices of the civil rights movement. There are counterexamples, to be sure, the most notable being *Brandenburg v. Ohio*, in which the Court extended the First Amendment to protect a Ku Klux Klan rally, but many of the most important First Amendment principles were developed in the context of protecting speech that the federal courts were at the time more inclined to love than to hate.

Contrast the Court's record during the civil rights movement with its decisions regarding communism during the long period when anticommunist hysteria gripped the nation. In the latter cases, which involved individuals whose speech the Court was more likely to hate, the Court upheld the imprisonment and deportation of Communist party members and, for the most part, failed to provide significant protection to political speech. First Amendment protections appear to be much easier to come by when the Court favors the speaker.

This history offers two reasons for caution concerning the First Amendment and abortion clinic protests. First, the opposition many pro-choice advocates have to Operation Rescue's point of view may lead them to be less than wholly vigilant in assessing the First Amendment risks of bringing federal laws like the Racketeer Influenced and Corrupt Organizations Act (RICO), the Freedom of Access to Clinic Entrances Act (FACE), and the Ku Klux Klan Act to bear on the actions of abortion clinic protesters. Second, the danger of establishing precedents that will come back to haunt progressive voices is especially high, given that today's federal judiciary, thanks to Presidents Reagan and Bush, has little sympathy for progressive causes and is often remarkably insensitive to First Amendment concerns. Therefore, I think it important that we carefully consider the First Amendment implications of some of the legal actions taken against abortion clinic protesters.

I

I want to begin with what is *not* a First Amendment concern in the regulation of abortion clinic protests. Operation Rescue and its defenders, like the boy who cried wolf, routinely invoke the First Amendment where no substantial constitutional concerns are merited. Just as routinely, these claims have been rejected. The first argument antiabortion protesters make is to characterize their protests as peaceful and nonviolent, akin to the civil rights protests of the 1960s. Pro-choice advocates sometimes get caught up in this argument by calling antiabortion protests violent, and there is no question that some antiabortion protesters have used violent means. But this exchange misses the point. Clearly some protesters are violent, but just as clearly many are not. The issue, however, is not violence, but the use of force. Even the "peaceful" use of force—as in a blockade—goes beyond any First Amendment protected speech. Antiabortion blockaders are not trying to persuade others to adopt their views through communication, but to physically compel them to do so by the force of numbers.

The second argument blockaders make, especially in the context of the clinic access bill, is that to punish abortion blockaders is to punish "thought crimes." This argument, which is identical to the one advanced against enhanced penalties for racially motivated assaults, cannot withstand scrutiny. Critics of FACE maintain that it is unconstitutionally selective because it punishes only those who use violence, force, or the threat of force *against persons seeking to obtain or facilitate an abortion.* Because the law does not punish those who use violence, force, or the threat of force for all other purposes, it is said to violate the First Amendment.

If this argument were accepted, it would mean not only that the clinic access laws are unconstitutional, but that a whole host of well-established federal antidiscrimination and civil rights laws are also unconstitutional. The clinic access bills are patterned after several federal laws that prohibit interference with the exercise of civil rights. For example, 18 U.S.C. §594 prohibits intimidation, threats, and coercion "for the purpose of interfering with the right of another person to vote or to vote as he may choose." Similarly, 18 U.S.C. §372 makes it unlawful to "conspire to prevent, by force, intimidation, or threat, any person from accepting or holding any office." Other laws prohibit interference by force or threat of force with the exercise of housing rights (42 U.S.C. §3631[a]), jury rights (18 U.S.C. §1503), and a range of civil rights (18 U.S.C. §245[b]). If FACE were unconstitutional because it selectively protects persons exercising their rights to obtain or provide abortions, then so, too, would be laws selectively protecting persons exercising their rights to vote, hold office, or enjoy equal housing opportunities.

II

Having identified what is *not* of First Amendment concern, I'd like to touch on three areas that may be of concern: (A) the specificity of FACE; (B) the steep penalties associated with FACE and other federal remedies like 42 U.S.C. §1985(3) and RICO; and (C) the difficulties of drawing lines between protected and proscribable conduct in abortion clinic protests.

A. Specificity of the Clinic Access Law

Unlike a general trespassing or interference with business ordinance, FACE focuses on a particular target: abortion clinics. Whenever a law singles out particular instances of a general form of expressive conduct for prohibition, there is at least the possibility that the particular conduct is being singled out because its message is politically unpopular. Thus, for example, a bill prohibiting flag burning is more constitutionally suspect than a bill prohibiting all public burnings.

The specificity of the clinic access law raises a legitimate question: Why is blocking access to abortion or reproductive health care clinics singled out? Couldn't a broader law, prohibiting blockades against any building, serve the same purposes? A broader bill might be politically unacceptable to progressives because of fears that it could apply to political actions by groups whose views they favor, such as ACT-UP, unions, minority groups, or environmental activists. But if that is the case, then perhaps the reason the clinic access law passed is precisely the unpopularity of Operation Rescue's cause rather than the objective character of its conduct. If so, First Amendment concerns are raised.

This concern was reflected quite explicitly in the original House version of the bill, which sought to exempt from its ambit "conduct by a party to a labor dispute in furtherance of labor or management objectives in that dispute" (H.R. 796, §248[d][2]). This language was apparently demanded by the labor movement, out of concern that union pickets might be subject to the act's sanctions. But extending that sort of exception to a politically favored group or cause is precisely what the First Amendment does not permit (see *Carey v. Brown*, 447 U.S. 455 [1979]; *Police Department of Chicago v. Mosley*, 408 U.S. 92 [1971]). The suspicion that arises from such selective *exceptions* is the flip side of the suspicion that should arise from selective *prohibition*, at least where the same goals might be accomplished through a general prohibition.

One might also ask whether the clinic access law is different from the bill criminalizing draft card destruction during the Vietnam War, which the Supreme Court upheld in a much-criticized opinion, *United States v. O'Brien*. The conduct criminalized in *O'Brien* was already unlawful; people were legally required to maintain their draft cards. Congress criminalized destruction and increased the penalties precisely in order to deter and punish antiwar protesters. The Supreme Court upheld the law by reasoning that it regulated conduct without any explicit reference to what the conduct communicated, but everyone knew that the real reason the law passed was because draft card burners were unpopular with the status quo.

The conduct prohibited by FACE is already prohibited under various state laws (such as trespass and interference with business relations). Why enact a special law for such conduct when directed against abortion clinics? Moreover, FACE dramatically raises the penalties for such already proscribed conduct. A trespass would be punishable by a one- to three-year prison sentence on the criminal side, and by punitive damages and $5,000 statutory damages on the civil side. Is this because Operation Rescue presents a special problem and has demonstrated by its actions the ineffectiveness of other remedies, or is it because Operation Rescue is a politically unpopular group? While there is substantial evidence that the law responds to the former, legitimate concern, it is certainly worth asking whether the latter played a part in the law's enactment.

B. Increased Penalties

Related concerns arise under the two existing federal statutes potentially available for use against Operation Rescue: the Ku Klux Klan Act (42 U.S.C. §1985[3]) and the Racketeer Influenced and Corrupt Organizations Act (18 U.S.C. §1961 *et seq.*). These laws are looked to (as is FACE) because they are more effective than state causes of action. Federal jurisdiction allows litigants to impose restrictions on Operation Rescue over a broader geographic area; §1985(3) provides for attorneys' fees; and RICO offers treble damages *and* attorneys' fees. These factors make such laws more effective at protecting women's rights, but also more effective at chilling political expression.

So far the debate concerning these laws has been statutory, not constitutional, in nature: how to construe their terms. But underlying those statutory construction questions are nascent First Amendment issues. The more broadly the laws are construed, the more available they are to respond to abortion clinic protests, but also the more available they are to respond to labor union actions and other political protests that progressives might favor.

1. Section 1985(3). The Supreme Court in *Bray v. Alexandria Women's Health Center* made it virtually impossible to use §1985(3)'s first clause against abortion blockaders. That clause prohibits conspiracies to deprive persons of equal protection of the laws. The question posed in *Bray* was whether the law could be applied to Operation Rescue. The Supreme Court held that it could not, at least under the facts presented by that case. Plaintiffs could have lost *Bray* in the Supreme Court on any number of grounds. Justice Scalia, writing for the majority, used the case to write an expansive opinion rejecting plaintiffs' claims on multiple grounds and making future use of this provision against abortion blockaders very unlikely.

First, the majority held that the statute requires a showing of class-based animus, and that Operation Rescue was motivated not by animus against women, but by animus against abortion. The latter, the Court held, did not constitute a class-based animus, reaffirming the ludicrous dichotomy that the Court first propounded in *Geduldig v. Aiello*, where it held that pregnancy discrimination did not constitute sex discrimination because the class of nonpregnant persons includes women as well as men.

Second, the Court held that a plaintiff in a §1985(3) case against private parties must show that the conspiracy was "aimed at" a constitutional right protected against private encroachment. Here, the woman's right to travel, one of the *only* constitutional rights protected against private action, was undeniably affected by Operation Rescue blockades, but the Court found that interference with that right wasn't Operation Rescue's purpose.

Third, the Court held that a claim based on the right to travel must allege a conspiracy to infringe *interstate* travel, which presumably can be shown either by demonstrating that the blockade was set up on the border itself (or perhaps on an interstate highway) or that the blockaders discriminatorily blocked travelers from out of state.

In light of how the majority dealt with the deprivation clause of §1985(3), probably the only favor they did the plaintiffs was *not* to reach the other claim in the case, based on the second clause of §1985(3), known as the "hindrance" clause. That clause applies to conspiracies "for the purpose of preventing or hindering the constituted authorities of any State or Territory from giving or securing to all persons within such State or Territory the equal protection of the laws." The majority said that claim was not properly raised. The hindrance clause of §1985(3) thus remains a potential ground for action against antiabortion protesters. In fact, four justices (Souter, Stevens, Blackmun, and O'Connor) indicated that the hindrance claim was properly raised and that a claim could be made out. With Justice Ginsburg replacing Justice White, there might well be five votes for a hindrance clause claim.

But while §1985(3)'s hindrance clause may still be available for actions against Operation Rescue, it may also be available for any conspiracy designed to frustrate police protection of another group's rights. Thus, efforts to picket and disrupt all-male or all-white associations could be covered, as could labor pickets, environmental direct actions, and other political demonstrations.

Here, again, the issue is whether progressives are willing to have the laws they invoke against Operation Rescue used against groups they might favor, be it an antinuclear or antiwar protest, a WHAM mobilization, or a labor picket. If we are not, that may suggest that Operation Rescue has some legitimate First Amendment concerns.

2. *RICO*. A similar issue underlies the RICO abortion clinic case the Supreme Court decided in January 1994, *NOW v. Scheidler*, which held that RICO can be applied to the Pro-Life Action Network (PLAN). The Seventh Circuit had dismissed a RICO suit against PLAN on the ground that RICO was intended to reach only enterprises that are economically motivated. The Supreme Court reversed, holding that RICO does not require any demonstration of economic motive.

The First Amendment implications raised by this statutory construction question are illustrated by the solicitor general's position in the *Scheidler* case. The United States opposed the economic motive requirement because it wants to be able to use RICO against "terrorist organizations." But who has the United States considered a terrorist organization? Its targets have included the African National Congress, the Palestine Liberation Organization, the Committee in Solidarity with the People of El Salvador, and so on—that is, many organizations that have legitimate political ends but also engage in some illegal activity.

Under the Court's ruling, RICO applies to any politically motivated "enterprise" that has engaged in two or more predicate acts over a ten-year period. Predicate acts include mail and wire fraud, which consists of any deception transmitted through mail or phone that results in harm to another. Another predicate act is extortion, which some courts have construed to include any demonstration that interrupts the normal course of business (transforming trespass into extortion into RICO). The fact that RICO turns on "enterprise" and "conspiracy" also raises associational rights concerns. Its potentially broad application to groups that have both lawful political objectives and unlawful objectives cannot be dismissed. Moreover, it triggers severe penalties: treble damages and attorneys' fees on the civil side (in one antiabortion protesters' case, $887 in actual damage to property resulted in a $68,000 RICO judgment, with treble damages and attorneys' fees), and forfeiture in the criminal context.

C. Distinguishing Lawful from Unlawful Activities

The final area of concern involves the dangers posed when the state seeks to regulate the unlawful activities of a group engaged in both lawful and unlawful activities. Operation Rescue has engaged in both lawful protest activities and unlawful acts such as blockades and trespass. Where both protected and unprotected conduct are intermingled, and where one seeks to hold individuals responsible for the acts of the organization, First Amendment lines are particularly important to draw.

NAACP v. Claiborne Hardware is the best guide. It requires "precision of regulation," which is easier said than done. *Claiborne Hardware* involved the NAACP's largely peaceful boycott of white-owned stores in Mississippi. There was some violence against those who didn't honor the boycott. The lower courts held the NAACP and boycott participants liable for all the merchants' losses. The Supreme Court reversed, holding that only those who took part in the violence could be held liable and that damages could be assessed only for injuries proximately caused by that violence.

The Court also set limits on penalties for speech by leaders in such a demonstration. Charles Evers, the NAACP field secretary, had said that boycott violators would be "disciplined" and that "if we catch any of you going in any of them racist stores, we're gonna break your damn neck." Citing *Brandenburg v. Ohio*, the Court held that such advocacy could not be penalized. The Court also held that the NAACP as an organization could not be held responsible unless it authorized or ratified the illegal activity.

But these lines are very difficult to draw in practice. When does advocacy become ratification? When does advocacy become conspiracy? Can the organization be penalized without injuring associational rights? Pro-choice advocates should carefully adhere to the guidelines set forth in *Claiborne Hardware* in framing the relief requested in actions against abortion blockaders. But there is real difficulty in applying them.

III

I'd like to close with a broader question: Should pro-choice advocates be committing so many resources to going after Operation Rescue? This is not technically a First Amendment matter, but rather a strategic one that might be informed by First Amendment history.

Experience demonstrates that attempts to censor as often as not have the paradoxical effect of increasing interest in the speech that the state seeks to suppress. The very fact that the state takes it so seriously makes others interested. Moreover, the image of people acting out of commitment against the state often gives their cause a certain moral weight in our culture.

Are pro-choice advocates doing the same thing in going after Operation Rescue? It cannot help but increase Operation Rescue's visibility and is likely to make certain people lean in their direction because they sympathize with individuals being harassed by the state: The image of committed men and women lying in the street and being pulled forcibly away by police is one that progressives have often used to garner support and attention for their causes. Do we contribute to that through these suits?

Do we have any other choice but to stand with the state? Perhaps not, but it shows the dilemma of having the law on your side.

■ **Sylvia Law**

In the area of clinic violence, there has been remarkably little conflict between the preservation of First Amendment rights and respect for women's rights to privacy and equality. The reason is that most pro-choice lawyers are also sophisticated champions of the First Amendment. Time and again pro-choice lawyers, representing clinics and women, and seeking protection for their clients against violence, have told judges that the First Amendment protects antichoice demonstrators.

A wonderful handbook from the ACLU Reproductive Freedom Project, *Preserving the Right to Choose: How to Cope with Violence and Disruption at Abortion Clinics*, advises clinics as to what they can do to protect their staff and patients. Substantively, it could as well be directed to the antichoice demonstrators, telling them what their rights are. As we all know, the law is often filled with ambiguity. It is unusual that a book advising one side in an ongoing dispute takes a substantive point of view that could just as well serve the disputants on the other side.

For example, in the section on "Coping with Specific Tactics, Picketing Outside Abortion Facilities," the handbook begins "peaceful picketing on public sidewalks adjacent to abortion clinics is protected by the First Amendment to the

Constitution and can never be prohibited." Now, I don't think that is an accurate statement of First Amendment law, because there are a lot of exceptions to the principle that peaceful picketing on public sidewalks can never be prohibited.[2] But certainly it is an interpretation of the Constitution that the ACLU supports and that protects the speech we hate.

As another example, the handbook points out that the people who call themselves sidewalk counselors often scream "baby-killer" at clinic patients as they approach the clinics, and wave blood-spattered dolls and pictures of dismembered fetuses in the women's faces. The booklet says: "However, name calling, debating and other offensive *purely verbal* tactics are fully protected by the First Amendment." Again, this is a view of the First Amendment that the ACLU supports, but not a fully accurate description of what the Court has, in fact, done.[3] Pro-choice advocates' sensitivity to First Amendment issues helps to assure that antichoice protesters are free to gather at clinics and require patients to pass through a mob of people shouting "murder" and waving pictures of fetuses at them. The only things prohibited are outright trespass, physical blockades, and assault, which are regular occurrences, as are bombings, arson, chemical attacks, and assaults on clinic personnel and their children.[4]

David Cole is surely right that it is vital to defend the speech we hate if we are going to being able to defend the speech we love. In part to be provocative I want to raise the question whether pro-choice civil libertarians have gone too far in respecting the rights of antichoice demonstrators. I want to defend the notion that, consistent with the First Amendment, the state could create a much larger bubble of privacy around abortion clinics.

The Supreme Court considered this question in 1978 in a case called *Beth Israel Hospital v. National Labor Relations Board*.[5] That case involved union claims to be able to solicit members within the hospital setting. Labor speech has traditionally enjoyed an enhanced form of protection under the First Amendment.[6] But despite the enhanced protection of labor speech, and despite the fact that pure speech was involved, a unanimous Supreme Court adopted the view that hospitals are different and speech in them can be limited to a greater degree. The Court held that serious concerns for patient welfare justify a prohibition on union solicitation in all patient care areas, including visitors' waiting rooms, corridors, and elevators used to transport patients. The justices were unanimous in support of the proposition that restrictions that couldn't be allowed elsewhere can and should be allowed in the hospital context.

As a health care advocate, I have often invoked the First Amendment to try to gain access to public facilities for the purpose of communicating with staff and patients about issues of concern to them. And, as a health care advocate, I am skeptical of the hospital's claim for a broad ban on union speech. Nonetheless, I also agree with *all* the justices in that case that the health care context is special. Restrictions that we might not countenance in other contexts are sometimes appropriate in the health care setting.

There are many situations in which the Supreme Court has held that speech rights must give way to other interests, even when the speech rights involve only peaceful picketing. For example, the Court upheld laws prohibiting all expressive picketing in front of courthouses,[7] as well as broad restrictions on peaceful picketing outside of public schools.[8]

We all know that polling places routinely prohibit solicitation and electioneering within a specified distance of the voting booth. While I disagree with the details of these decisions, the notion that it is legitimate to create a bubble of tranquillity within which certain important functions can take place seems to me sound. At least it is the law.

Women seeking abortions and the staff that serve them deserve at least as much tranquillity, privacy, and protection as schoolchildren, judges, and hospital patients. They do not now receive it. In failing to fight for and provide protection for abortion clinics at the local level, we have been driven to invoke some more esoteric federal remedies, like RICO. Cole is correct in observing that these remedies raise their own serious problems. Nonetheless, given the persistence of the antichoice movement and the limitations on local law enforcement, federal intervention in some form remains essential to protect women's basic right to choice. The federal Freedom of Access to Clinic Entrances Act (FACE), adopted in 1994, provides some protection, but following our traditional pattern of deference to First Amendment issues, it is highly limited.[9] I would go further and try to create a bubble of privacy and tranquillity around abortion clinics.

In 1994, the Supreme Court upheld a state court injunction that imposed a thirty-six-foot buffer zone and noise restrictions around an abortion clinic.[10] The majority held that noise "control is particularly important around hospitals and medical facilities during surgery and recovery periods."[11] The court reversed a provision of the injunction that prohibited the display of images observable inside the clinic within three hundred feet of the facility. "[I]t is much easier for the clinic to pull its curtains than for a patient to stop up her ears, and no more is required to avoid seeing the placards through the windows of the clinic."[12]

At the level of principle, it seems the court has struck a reasonable balance between the needs of clinic patients and the rights of protesters. At the level of daily practice, these struggles continue.

■ Catherine Albisa

In many respects, the potential conflict between the free speech rights of antichoice individuals and organizations and a woman's right to choose abortion has been exaggerated. When you work with clinics, you discover that when clinic personnel feel they need protection, it is not speech about which they are primarily concerned. Clinics are constantly faced with threats of physical violence to personnel and their families, bombings, arsons, blockades, destruction of property, butyric acid attacks, the tying up of phone lines for hours or days on end (so women cannot call in—including women who may be having problems from a recent abortion, such as infection or bleeding), stalking, and intense harassment. Moreover, the recent murders at clinics have naturally further heightened anxiety over physical safety.

Thus, the majority of antichoice conduct over which clinic personnel are concerned involves no speech at all, and even when speech is involved it is usually of the type (i.e., threats) that clearly is not constitutionally protected. The instances where there is real conflict between free speech rights and the ability of clinics to provide safe health care constitute only a small part of the problem.

Moreover, while speech is often intermingled with illegal conduct, the presence of protected speech does not immunize that conduct. For public safety reasons, environmentalists are prohibited from walking across a crowded highway in Los Angeles and stopping cars in political protest. Additionally, no one would argue that an abusive partner who is stalking a woman from whom he is separated is insulated from the law because he starts spouting a sexist ideology as he stalks her. Indeed, the ability of courts to issue temporary restraining orders for women who have been abused in the past or who have been stalked or harassed is unquestionable. Clinic violence and harassment present similar issues. There is a history of violence and illegal acts, and clinics seek protection and request orders keeping the perpetrators at a distance.

One significant difference, however, is that clinics need protection from many individuals and organizations, all of which are not readily identifiable, making the crafting of a remedy far more complicated. Any such remedy is inevitably going to constrain or at least inhibit persons who have not engaged in proscribable behavior. For example, buffer zones that require protesters to remain a specific number of feet from the clinic entrance have been created by courts to protect physical access to a clinic. Since this legal remedy applies equally to those who intend only to communicate ideas and to those who intend to block access, a buffer zone incidentally infringes on speech.

The Supreme Court has upheld at least one such buffer zone in *Madsen v. Women's Health Center, Inc.*[13] In that case a buffer zone of thirty-six feet was imposed by an injunction, and the Court created a new standard of review for injunctions more stringent than the standard of review for content-neutral statutes.[14] Despite the more stringent standard, the Court still found that the buffer zone was constitutional.[15]

Other injunctive remedies that are designed to ensure access to clinics or prevent harassment, but that also as a by-product infringe on speech, include restrictions on noise outside of clinics, and a variety of "no approach" zones where protesters are prohibited from approaching patients within a certain number of feet from the clinic. *Madsen* upheld a noise restriction and made clear that any reasonably tailored noise restriction would meet constitutional requirements. *Madsen* struck down as too broad a no-approach zone of three hundred feet. Other proposed no-approach zones vest the "right" in the patient: a protester may approach a patient, but if that patient requests that the protester remain at a distance then the protester must back off for a designated number of feet (in one proposal eight feet was suggested).

While *Madsen* addresses many of the questions relating to clinic access and speech, the universe of constitutionally permissible remedies to protect clinic access has yet to be demarcated. In particular, what remedies are constitutionally permissible when antichoice groups engage in verbal harassment that falls short of threats still poses the most difficult question. It is in this context that free speech rights and the right to privacy come closest to clashing.

Mediating Theories

It is generally recognized that when conflicts arise among constitutional rights, it is necessary to balance the competing interests at stake. The U.S. Constitution is an organic document without rigid absolutes, and its very structure is inconsistent with an analysis that would permit one right to be absolutely protected at the expense of eviscerating another.

Constitutional analysis requires that the document be read, to the extent possible, as internally consistent, and provides for reasonable jurisprudential responses to difficult conflicts. Moreover, any constitutional right is also limited by the need for public safety and order. Although that concept has been abused and should be applied to restrict constitutional rights only when absolutely necessary (i.e., when there are no other "narrower" means to ensure public order and safety), it is not a controversial proposition that the boundaries of these rights are often determined by public safety considerations.

One example involving both competing rights and public safety issues is historical (and current to varying degrees): the organized resistance by white supremacists to voting rights for African Americans. Such resistance often included coercive verbal threats directed at African Americans exercising their right to vote. These threats were definitely speech, and they also, in most cases, communicated political racist messages. However, although the First Amendment protects even the most offensive speech, it is beyond question that First Amendment protections did not extend to white supremacist conspiracies to deprive U.S. citizens of another constitutional right. If protections were absolute simply because speech was involved, groups such as the Ku Klux Klan could effectively eviscerate the right to vote for huge numbers of people. Moreover, the atmosphere of violence created by this conspiracy to deprive citizens of voting posed a threat to the public safety.

We are presented with an analogous situation regarding the tactics employed by antiabortion extremists. As in the voting rights context, the Constitution recognizes that a general balancing is necessary if we are going to further all the substantial and important rights provided by the Constitution, which necessarily include reproductive rights.

Once we accept the general principle that rights must be balanced, the questions we face are what type of mediating theories are available to us, and what factors to take into account when we formulate such theories. At the very minimum, any theory must consider that disparate constitutional rights share certain common goals, all of which advance the underlying values and principles of the entire document. Such common goals include assuring all citizens equal participation in society, self-determination, and the ability to express oneself. Although the core principles remain the same, the goals are advanced through different means, depending on which right is at issue. For example, the rights to free speech, privacy, and equality all advance the principles of self-determination and equal participation in society. Speech is a critical means of participating equally in society, and, as has been noted by the Supreme Court in *Planned Parenthood of Southeastern Pennsylvania v. Casey*, privacy rights guaranteeing childbirth choices are critical for women's equal participation in society. Moreover, making childbirth choices is as essential a way to express oneself as standing on a soapbox.

An ideal theory would interpret and define constitutional rights to advance all of these common goals. It becomes complicated when the manner in which one right is being exercised impinges on the ability of other citizens to either exercise the same or another equally important constitutional right. In such instances, power relations must be considered or any analysis takes place in a vacuum. Sexual harassment is one example. Sexual harassment can, and often does, consist solely of speech directed by a man toward a woman. (Theoretically, it can also consist of speech by a woman toward a man, a man toward a man, or a woman toward a woman, as well as scenarios involving transsexuals. But realistically the significant and pervasive problem of which we as a society are aware is harassment directed at women by men. Indeed, if the practical problem were a different one the "power relations" factor of the analysis would also be completely different.) Moreover, sexual harassment often involves giving women "political" messages that they do not belong in the workplace. Despite any political content or speech involved, sexual harassment in the workplace can be prohibited without violating the First Amendment.

Finding that sexual harassment can be constitutionally prohibited is consistent with advancing the Constitution's underlying principles and goals. While sexual harassment permits men to express themselves, considering existing power relations between genders, the legitimate value of such speech is greatly outweighed by the harm it does to equality. Indeed, without the ability to work equal participation by women in society becomes impossible. Moreover, any impingement on men's ability to express themselves is quite limited, as they can still express themselves outside of the work environment, or they can express their views even in the work environment without engaging in sexual harassment or creating a hostile work environment. Such factors should be considered when constitutional goals conflict.

Violence and Harassment Directed at Clinics

The same considerations need to be taken into account when considering remedies against clinic violence and harassment. As in the sexual harassment context, the power dynamics favor the harasser. The patient must go to the clinic or forgo exercising her constitutional right to abortion. She usually walks in alone or with one person, while being surrounded by hostile protesters. She is in both an emotionally and a physically vulnerable position. The history of violence surrounding clinic protests would cause any reasonable patient to feel intimidated and frightened. In sum, this atmosphere has a far higher likelihood of producing fear than dialogue.

If antichoice groups succeed in closing clinics down through violence and intimidation, in practical terms there is no other avenue for women to exercise their right to choose an abortion. However, if such groups are enjoined or prohibited from harassing patients within a certain number of feet from the clinic, or are prohibited from impeding access, there are still numerous alternatives to convey their political message. Moreover, the communicative value of harassment is outweighed by the damage to privacy and health interests, particularly when the same message can be communicated in less destructive ways.

Thus, constitutional values would be better served by prohibiting harassment. The values at issue are free expression, bodily autonomy, and medical privacy. Both the women patients and the protesters are engaging in expressive acts. The patients are also making life-directing decisions that have significant health, social, and personal consequences. The ability to make these decisions is necessary for a patient to maintain her bodily autonomy and medical privacy. Limiting the expressive acts of the protesters to a sphere excluding harassment would have a minimal impact on their ability to convey their message, but it would have a substantial impact on their ability to coerce women.

The fundamental problem that remains is what constitutes "harassment." Much of the activity outside of clinics today is easy to classify as harassment (particularly the screaming at and surrounding of patients as they attempt to enter the clinic). However, there will always be gray areas that are cause for concern to all of us interested in free expression's being vigorously protected. Whether a particular act constitutes harassment will usually depend on the context, so it is a problem that must be addressed on a case-by-case basis.

Access to Health Care or Content-based Discrimination?

David Cole asked if we are treating Operation Rescue differently because we do not like the organization. The question, however, of whether we are treating clinics differently because of this very tense and combative atmosphere in which we find ourselves is equally legitimate. Would we put up with that type of behavior outside a cardiac surgery unit? Would we permit cardiac patients who are undergoing surgery to be subjected to such tremendous disturbances and to have their health jeopardized? Such activity outside a cardiac unit would be stopped by the authorities immediately. Moreover, it would not engender much controversy. Indeed, there are reasons clinics need even more protection than hospitals from harassing activities. As Sylvia Law pointed out, hospitals are generally very large buildings so that patients are more insulated from activities outside. But a clinic is smaller than many people's homes, and you cannot protect the patients if you have a mob outside. Patients arrive for surgery with elevated blood pressure and other symptoms during blockades and loud, harassing protests. Regardless of how we approach this problem, we must always take into account that necessary medical care is being imperiled, and that the women affected are about to undergo surgery. Some have said that because we are singling out access for clinics, it must be the ideas of the protesters that legislatures and courts are trying to repress.[16] It is far more likely, however, that the motivation, in Congress and state legislatures and by advocacy groups, is to stop the coercion and violence and ensure women's health. This debate would be far better served by draining it of such hyperbole regarding sinister motives and repression, and instead focusing on how legitimately to protect any health care facility. Too much attention has been focused on a narrow area of perceived conflict, rather than the more serious problem of ensuring access to safe health care.

Remedies

Thus far, women and clinics have sought three general types of protection.[17] In *Bray v. Alexandria Women's Health Clinic*, clinics attempted to seek protection under tradition civil rights laws by arguing that antichoice groups were conspiring to deprive women of their constitutional rights, but the Supreme Court rejected their claims.[18] Clinics have also availed themselves of RICO and sued antichoice groups for extortion. Although the use of RICO has alarmed many civil rights groups, RICO requires predicate acts of extortion, arson, murder, and so forth, which are far outside the purview of the First Amendment. Additionally, clinics have relied on state laws prohibiting trespass and destruction of property. Courts issuing injunctions on these laws have crafted some creative solutions that safeguard speech, such as injunctions that allow a protester to approach a woman but require the protester to back off for eight feet if the woman so requests. This gives the woman space to get to the clinic, while the protester can certainly still be heard.

Regardless of the remedy upon which a clinic and its women patients ultimately rely, it is inevitable that some speech that is problematic and disturbing will be protected. Speech itself, however, is not going to eliminate access. Legitimate speech does not pose the kind of problems that close down clinics. Nor is there anything problematic about a woman who legitimately changes her mind, because the ultimate goal is choice and self-determination.

Conclusion

While there are some hard questions regarding verbal harassment in this context, there are potential solutions that still provide an opportunity for the antichoice message to get out, but eliminate the threatening atmosphere in which women now must seek health care. Clinics and women have primarily been confronted with force, threats of force, and invasions of privacy that have traditionally been protected by tort law (i.e., revealing private information at the workplace and/or intentionally inflicting emotional distress). That these activities are not constitutionally protected is not a new concept created by pro-choice advocacy groups.

The most disturbing aspect of this debate is that a few areas of conflict between speech and privacy have received a tremendous amount of attention, while the crises created by this surge of criminality by middle-aged people laying on the ground has not been adequately addressed. Despite their middle-class appearance these anti-abortion protesters engage in criminal acts. Their cloak of religiosity and "family values," however, has created a problem in terms of public perception. The public has been slow to grasp that the campaigns initiated by these organizations are in large part based on criminal activity.[19] Moreover, antichoice groups have used the First Amendment to obfuscate further the real underlying, unacceptable, dangerous, and illegal behaviors of their movement.

■ Discussion

STEVEN R. SHAPIRO: I completely agree that the Constitution does not protect threats of violence properly defined, and that someone does not gain immunity for illegal activity, either because that illegal activity is ideologically motivated or because in the course of that illegal activity somebody is simultaneously engaging in speech.

Having said that, there are two very different kinds of problems that we have to address candidly. One is what could be called in traditional First Amendment terms time, place, and matter regulations. Are we going to put limits on the number of people who can be outside of abortion clinics? Are we going to somehow try to regulate the noise of the protest? Are we going to create a bubble around abortion clinics, as Sylvia Law suggests, that requires people to be a certain distance back? Will we have the sort of rules that Cathy Albisa was talking about, where you can approach somebody, but when they say no, you have to back off?

Those can be thorny problems, but they are not unique to abortion clinics and can be worked out and reconciled in the way that courts and advocates have been dealing with time, place, and matter regulations in First Amendment cases for many years. There is some validity to Sylvia's point that hospitals and clinics have been treated as different for many years by the courts because of the nature of the activity going on inside and the legitimate need not only to protect the privacy of the people involved, but for a certain amount of peace and quiet so that the work that is going on inside can go on uninterrupted. On the other hand, I am a little nervous about relying on cases like *Cox v. Louisiana*, which upheld the ban on picketing in front of courthouses, because I think that is an inappropriate rule in a society that should allow people to criticize what is going on in courtrooms as long as they do not do so in a disruptive way. The Court itself has backed off from that ruling at least slightly in cases like *United States v. Grace*. Does a concept like "bubbles" mean you could not have one or two or three people standing outside an abortion clinic with a poster containing a picture of a supposedly aborted fetus that people would have to confront if they went inside? Maybe yes and maybe no. And the harsh reality of the situation is that whatever rules we create, whatever we say to people about limiting the number of protesters or putting them at a certain distance away from the abortion clinics, it is not working because the protesters are ignoring the rules, and the police are having to come in and get them out of the way. We're having counterprotests and protective chains created around abortion clinics, and the level of confrontation is simply rising.

My expectation is that it will continue to rise, especially if, as appears likely, the core holding of *Roe* is unlikely to be overturned by the Court any time in the near future. The battleground has become the battleground over the practical availability of abortions, not the legal and constitutional protection provided to abortions. And that has emboldened the antichoice movement and energized the pro-choice movement. The protest tactics are becoming more aggressive and the legal response is becoming more aggressive.

For me, the most difficult First Amendment issues are posed not by questions such as do you have to be fifty feet away as opposed to twenty feet away, but by what sort of legal remedies one can obtain in court against groups like Operation Rescue and others. In that context, David Cole has identified some very difficult issues for us to grapple with. The question of whether RICO requires an economic motive is interesting to people who are RICO junkies, but beyond that, what should raise some flags for First Amendment folks is the fact that RICO provides very onerous penalties, both criminal and civil, including treble damages that are clearly intended to be punitive. We have to ask ourselves about the appropriateness of imposing what are essentially punitive damages against organizations that undoubtedly engage in some unlawful activities but simultaneously are engaged in some lawful and constitutionally protected activities, and whether any remedy that goes beyond compensation is an appropriate remedy in a First Amendment context. Issues of injunctive remedies in this context are also very difficult. Can you use the fact that Operation Rescue has engaged in certain unlawful activities in City A as a basis for obtaining an injunction against their activities when they arrive in City B—but before they've ever done anything—based upon their past history of similar protests? Maybe yes, maybe no—but I think it is a difficult question to confront in First Amendment terms.

When we start getting away from time, place, and matter restrictions and we start talking about suing people for civil liability and making them pay damages, we have to be candid in acknowledging that while we have legal standards that we can all cite that tell us what the rules are, those lines are appropriately often very difficult to draw in the real world. In particular, the line between advocacy and incitement is notoriously difficult. To use one very real example, what do you do about the person who writes the pamphlet telling you how to blockade an abortion clinic and does not actually then go out and blockade the abortion clinic, but someone else reading the pamphlet then uses the tactics described to engage in the blockade. Is the person who wrote the pamphlet responsible? Is the organization that published the pamphlet responsible? As David Cole asked, would we be prepared to apply those same rules against other groups?

My final point, which goes beyond the narrow issue of abortion blockades and abortion protests, has to do with content-neutrality. Is the proposed federal law on clinic access content-neutral? Can we have a law that prohibits you from blockading abortion clinics but doesn't prohibit you from blockading other public buildings? If we have such a law can we exempt labor pickets from what would otherwise be a general ban? This highlights the increasing confusion and ambiguity in our general First Amendment law of content-neutrality that surfaced in Justice Scalia's opinion in *RAV v. City of St. Paul* about hate speech. The whole debate about abortion clinics is going to force us to reexamine a number of basic First Amendment premises, including the meaning and limits of doctrine on content-neutrality, when it applies and when it doesn't apply. This debate is going to shape our sense of the First Amendment in the coming years.

SYLVIA LAW: I found it surprising that David Cole and Steve Shapiro posed the content-neutrality point as if to ask, If we're going to prohibit blockades at abortion clinics, shouldn't we also prohibit them at all buildings? I think that's a misleading way to characterize the problem. I could see a certain advantage in having an antiblockade law that covers all health care facilities rather than simply all abortion clinics. But, on the other hand, you always hate to enact federal regulations to deal with a problem that doesn't exist. There's not a real big blockade problem at open-heart surgery units; there's only a blockade problem at abortion clinics. It's not clear to me that it reflects a content bias when you try to address the problem that exists and not try to deal with problems that don't exist. But if you want to go broader, protecting all public buildings would just be a silly law.

SHAPIRO: I agree with you that there is no First Amendment problem with singling out a location and a problem that has arisen in a context where you are presumptively dealing with activity that is not First Amendment-protected activity. My point was that the legal doctrine in that area is now more confused than it has been for some time, and that one of the things that has emboldened people to raise content-based arguments against the federal law is the Supreme Court's opinion in *RAV v. City of St. Paul*. The whole issue is now, I think, in a state of some doctrinal ambiguity, and this is one of the real-life scenarios that's going to force the Court to come to grips with the confusion they have now sown.

CATHERINE ALBISA: Although there is a lot of focus on blockades and what actually goes on outside the clinics, that is becoming less of a problem than what goes on away from the clinics: the targeting of clinic personnel. This new strategy is driving people out of the field altogether. How do efforts to stop stalking and harassment intersect with First Amendment issues? Those laws are harder to draft than blockade laws. Also, I believe focusing on clinics is more protective of First Amendment rights than making general laws or forcing clinics to resort to general laws, such as RICO, which have fewer boundaries and weren't drafted with First Amendment concerns in mind.

QUESTION: With respect to Sylvia Law's "bubble of tranquillity," what if we had a situation where a health clinic is the medical equivalent of Denny's restaurant and had been reputed to mistreat African Americans and exclude them, and protesters wanted to protest that? Would your bubble of tranquillity work in the same way in that situation?

LAW: Well, I made the proposal partly to be provocative, and I'm not entirely sure to what extent I agree with it. But to defend it, I don't think it's necessarily troubling to say that the people who want to protest against the racist clinic have to do it a block away. There is a real interest in having the little bubble of tranquillity even if they're pursuing racist policies in providing their health care. It's not clear to me that it's unreasonable to say the protest can't take place right on the clinic steps even if it's expressing an idea that we would all want to see people protected and express.

CAROLYN SIMPSON: Maybe none of us want to think it's part of the problem, at least for the ACLU, but I think we have to acknowledge that there's a lot of sexism underlying all of this. These are *abortion* clinics we're talking about. This has to do with women's freedom of choice. Sure, some of these protesters engaging in criminal activities are also engaging in protected activities. Probably so are the people who violate the RICO laws in the more traditional economic way. No one has a corner on engaging in both criminal and noncriminal activities. The federal legislation probably wouldn't be as close to enactment if you hadn't had a male doctor shot. The ACLU really should examine itself and think: Wait a minute, if the people inside those clinics were men, the whole response would be different.

DIANNE CURTIS: I've been threatened with arrest several times, not for blockading a clinic, but for defending clinics. This exchange seems incredibly academic to me, as someone who spent a lot of time outside the clinics, because regardless of the laws that are already in existence, including criminal trespass laws, they're not implemented in any way that would guarantee access to clinics for women seeking abortions or other health care. I'd like to hear about the lack of implementation of content-neutral laws such as criminal trespass laws.

ALBISA: We wouldn't be in the position we were in if existing laws had been enforced adequately. In fact, protesters have broken into a physician's office, stopped everything going on there, and the police have responded by saying, "Well, that's public property." Inside the office. By the equipment. So the very reason we need legislation specifically directed at this problem is because there has been no neutrality in enforcement.

SHAPIRO: There is obviously a big problem with enforcement of the laws, and there are a variety of answers to that.

44   Discussion

One answer may be the use of §1985(3), the hindrance clause, that was left unresolved in *Bray*. I don't believe the ACLU has been coopted on the issue. In fact, the ACLU has been quite vigorous in calling not only on local authorities to step in and protect the right of women to reproductive choice, but on the federal government to intervene and play a much more active role. We have supported the clinic access bill and called on the Justice Department to bring in the FBI to protect doctors and clinics around the country from the escalating climate of violence.

It is also true that the lack of enforcement of the current laws has understandably and predictably led the abortion rights movement to ever more creative, inventive, and aggressive legal responses. And I don't think we can take the position that any legal response in pursuit of the right to reproductive freedom which we otherwise support is automatically an appropriate response because it is designed to protect rights that we advocate. There is some point down the road where the solution to one problem can create another problem, and it seems to me that that is an appropriate role for the ACLU to play, to point out when we think that point has been reached.

L A W : I want to respond to David Cole's questions about whether we devote too much resource and attention to the clinic violence area. I think we devote too much resource to abortion, period. In 1973, when the Supreme Court declared that abortion was legal, we should have started training doctors to do them and providing them and moved on to other things. I am so bored with abortion! But given the reality of the lack of training, and the quite understandable reluctance of physicians to work in places where they have to put up with this stuff, I just don't see what the alternative is except to keep fighting and trying to get more federal resources into the law enforcement aspect of the problem.

But even if we completely solve that problem, there still wouldn't be abortions available in most parts of the country because there aren't doctors being trained to do them. And so it's a multifaceted problem. As boring as it is, and as tired as we are of working on it, we just don't have realistic alternatives except to just keep plugging away.

SHAPIRO: If abortion was simply a legal or constitutional issue, as Sylvia says, it would have ended in 1973. But it's a political issue, too. And one of the judgments that any local police department makes when deciding how to allocate its resources is how the community demands that the resources be allocated. That is in many ways a political judgment as much as anything else and continues to require political organizing as much as lawyering.

ALBISA: The problems reinforce each other, because only 17 percent of the counties in the United States have abortion providers. That makes it easier for those who are trying to shut down clinics to concentrate in one area, and it makes it harder for women to go elsewhere because it's too far away, which then makes it easier to overload or overcome the local law enforcement.

JACK BETALIA: Going back to the speech we love/speech we hate issue, while David Cole was describing the *NOW v. Scheidler* case, I was searching my memory for the details of a case back in the 1970s in which the applicable federal statute was the Sherman Act and not RICO. The issue, as I remember it, was whether boycott activity which was directed to a political end—specifically passage of the ERA—could be subject to penalty under the Sherman Act. The defendant in that case was NOW, the plaintiff in the RICO case, and it reminded me that very much the same economic versus political dichotomy was at issue in that case.

In the Sherman Act context, the Supreme Court has found it necessary to fashion an exception informed by First Amendment considerations, and there may very well have to be similar attention to other federal statutes initially directed toward economic activity. The ultimate point of my comment is that the distinction is one of some significance when it comes to using statutes that were initially designed for other purposes.

SHAPIRO: I agree with that. But I also think one could easily imagine a situation where you had a rule of law that said the antitrust laws could not be applied to a national organization like NOW that organizes economic boycotts in the hope of persuading states to ratify a proposed constitutional amendment. That activity ought not to be covered by the statute, and indeed ought to be constitutionally protected. It's a very big leap to go from there to saying that we ought to have similar concerns about a statute that reaches out and says that someone who commits two violent acts as part of an ongoing conspiratorial effort nonetheless ought to be insulated from federal legislation because those criminal acts were prompted by an ideological motive.

SIMPSON: I think it might be useful to the public at large if the ACLU came out very vocally and said, "You know, if it ever gets to the point where Operation Rescue is just engaging in speech activities, protected speech activities, then we have a possible civil liberties clash here. But right now, they're not. We're not talking about an organization that's engaged in protected speech activities. When they do, we'd be happy to talk to them." I think you can help define the problem for the American people and for the legislatures because people do look to the ACLU for guidance on speech.

GARA LAMARCHE: I'd like Catherine Albisa to expand on her assertion that increasingly the problems are in the realm of personal harassment, threats, and physical violence.

ALBISA: There is a different set of speech problems in terms of when we're defining what behavior and conduct we want stopped and what remedy we want in order to stop them. I'll give you examples. The antichoice movement has focused on Central Florida a lot, in part because the local law enforcement authorities don't respond. They go where the police officers don't respond. They focus on doctors who provide services in geographical areas where there are few doctors. They will put up "wanted" posters in the hotels, which are fairly threatening, with an underlying threat of force. While it's a closer question than blockades, it's not as problematic as what they do once the doctor arrives, which is to flood the lobby, not in any way that makes the operation of the hotel impossible, but surrounding the physician and harassing and threatening him or her. To the extent that there are threats of force involved, they're not protected. But what about the epithets? What if they start limiting their campaign to the kind of harassment where it's hard to establish if there's a threat of force involved? And what if physicians start leaving the field because of that? Right now, physicians are leaving the field because they're afraid to die, or because their property is being destroyed, or because their kids are threatened.

LAMARCHE: One of the interesting problems is that you don't have to in any meaningful legal way advocate violence in order to make it clear that somebody is marked. It's like the attacks on moderate Cuban exiles in Miami. Nobody goes on the radio saying, Go out and murder that person. They call him a "worm" or a Castroite traitor, and the people out there listening to those signals know exactly what they're supposed to do.

JUDITH RESNIK: I have a question about the framing of the question. I feel we've spent a good deal of time focusing on the protesters and Operation Rescue, and less focusing on people seeking to either give or get abortions. And I wonder, if the question had been asked from a civil liberties and civil rights perspective, what would the conversation be? What if we began with the problems of people who hope to be able to provide abortions, or related services, and women who want to get them. We'd be having a different conversation. We're already in a conversation of apology and haven't spent much time hearing about the First Amendment rights of a host of other people in this story.

SHAPIRO: I don't want to confuse how this debate was framed with the work and agenda of the ACLU. Because everyone knows that the ACLU has devoted tremendous time, energy, and resources over twenty years or more to protecting the right of women to reproductive freedom, in maintaining clinic access, and in protecting people's meaningful right to obtain abortions in the real world.

LAW: Well, I'll defend the ACLU here because the truth is the bulk of the work of the ACLU and of the Center for Reproductive Law and Policy is proactive, concerned most centrally with funding. Even though we lost the big fight on funding, that's a fight that's continued to be fought in state courts, with some success. In the Congress, every year it seems like we have two or three more votes for . . . What did we win this year? I think rape and incest, right? Whoopee. The second major issue, which is harder to address in legal terms, is the whole access question. Why aren't doctors trained to provide abortions? Why aren't most medical students even given the opportunity to learn how to do abortions? Why don't regular doctors who see pregnant women have to refer women to abortion services just like they have to refer them if they need a chest x-ray or a CAT scan? How is it that the medical culture has allowed abortion to become so marginalized that only the most heroic and self-sacrificing people will have anything whatsoever to do about it? It's really more about how do you create a campaign to change the culture. We're just not as good at that as we are at going into court and asserting a negative right. But I do think, to their credit, that the organizations understand that that's the agenda and are pursuing that agenda.

ALBISA: One possible way the issue could have been framed, which dealt with all the same questions, is how we can formulate effective constitutional legislative and judicial remedies to ensure access. The focus is then on the clinics: what can we do as opposed to what can't we do.

LAMARCHE: We framed it this way because this is a community of people—ACLU, Human Rights Watch, etc.—who share very strongly held common values. This is not a debate about abortion rights, because we're all strong supporters of abortion rights, and strong supporters of racial and gender equality. But it is characteristic of civil libertarians as a minority group in this society, despite their strong support for all those things, to be concerned about those issues on the margins that involve the rights of people who we don't like or that we hate. And it seemed to us that the consensus was becoming shakier as we went along. It was precisely because people like myself within the American Civil Liberties Union were finding that there was a strong body of opinion out there that because we were listening to and incorporating some of the other voices, we were departing from support for the First Amendment.

RESNIK: One of my concerns is that we are being drawn into the conversation that's very familiar and comfortable, and being distracted from a very difficult conversation which will probably raise similar kinds of concerns, but we don't even have the words for yet. And all along we are not serving the interests of people who desperately need to have their interests served, because in fact the decline of access in this area has a very sad history. I therefore think that when we are in this conversation we have to ask, How do we get there? Whose media questions and comments prompt us to be here? Is this the kind of conversation we want to be in, among people who all care about these issues a good deal? Why are we not thinking of the new right to travel and the new right to welfare, and some of those other new rights, as constitutional rights and civil liberties questions?

ALBISA: Something we lose sight of is what right is at risk right now. It's not as if Operation Rescue's ability to express itself were actually at risk, and the right to have an abortion were not. And we have to keep in mind that in terms of the practical realities, their expression, at least at this moment, is not much at risk. They are heard loud and clear in a lot of places, while the actual ability to act on the constitutional right to choose is very much at risk on a very practical level, particularly for low-income women.

■ PART TWO

Hate Crimes/Hate Speech

■ Ira Glasser

It is a fundamental mistake to think of speech and equality as being in conflict. It's a problem derivative of the way the question has been framed recently by lots of people in this society, and by the way we have been forced to respond to it. The notion that this is a zero-sum game, that the gains for one right can only come at the expense of the other, is a new concept, one that is dangerous to both rights and needs to be challenged.

That is not to say that there aren't conflicts and tensions between those two rights, predominantly at the margins in particular situations. But that is something very different from there being a fundamental conflict in a serious and profound way between the two rights. The notion that two or more rights come into conflict with each other at various points, mostly along the margins, is not new or particularly unique to this area. As a multi-issue organization, the ACLU spends a lot of its time confronting the tensions and conflicts between and among the various rights that we support. This problem is not unique to the First and Fourteenth Amendments. There are conflicts between the double jeopardy principle and civil rights enforcement that emerge over legal fictions like the dual sovereignty doctrine, as recently exemplified in the Rodney King trial.

There are conflicts between the right of reporters to obtain arrest records of people who have not been convicted and the privacy rights of such people not to have arrests disclosed. Anyone who has read Justice Douglas's dissent in *Wisconsin v. Yoder* knows that there are heart-rending and difficult conflicts between the religious rights of minors and the religious rights of their parents—questions of where does the state intervene, and if the state intervenes to protect the rights of one, how does it avoid intruding upon the rights of the other.

There are conflicts even within the First Amendment, of which religious freedom is the perfect example—endless tensions between the establishment clause and the free exercise clause. There are conflicts between parental rights normally to make important and consequential medical decisions about their minor children, and the right of minors to abortions without parental consent. There is hardly an area of constitutional rights that does not present conflicts and tensions between and among rights.

To suggest that there is something unique or fundamental in the area of First and Fourteenth Amendment rights different from the generic problem of rights in conflict disserves both rights and sets up a framework in which we appear to be forced to choose between one and the other: Which precedes which? Which trumps which? Which comes first? Which is more important? That is not the way to look at it for a variety of reasons, which I will address later.

The underlying problem, particularly on college campuses, that gives rise to this whole debate is the persistence of bigotry and discrimination and prejudice against racial minorities, against women, against gays and lesbians. The

First Amendment problem arises out of attempts—mostly misguided, dysfunctional, and unproductive—to remedy the problem of bigotry and discrimination and prejudice by enacting codes and rules that restrict speech that is reflective of that bigotry and discrimination. The First Amendment problem in that sense is derivative of the unresolved and underlying problem of bigotry and discrimination. It is impossible to get into this question in a way that has any analytic integrity without understanding that. The First Amendment problem would simply never arise if the underlying problem of bigotry and discrimination were not so persistent and ubiquitous, and the real questions are: Is curbing speech a permissible remedy? Is it functional? What else are we leaving unaddressed? It is important to think about those two problems together because that is how they occur in the real world.

Taken by itself, the First Amendment problem is not in the end very interesting or very different from First Amendment line-drawing that we do all the time, that we had to do during the antiwar and civil rights protests of the 1960s and 1970s. Those kind of line-drawing problems are hard, but they really are at the margins of the underlying problem. And in the end, they're not very different or legally very interesting. It's easy to say, for example, that the use of words themselves does not confer First Amendment immunity upon action and conduct that can be sanctioned. Extortion uses words; blackmail uses words. Nobody would suggest that a racially and/or sexually threatening phone call to a black co-ed in the middle of the night on a college campus is protected by the First Amendment. So, the notion that words themselves necessarily create a First Amendment immunity for conduct that is legitimately actionable must, I think, at the outset be rejected.

For example, I did not see that Sol Wachtler raised a First Amendment defense to anything he was charged with, and yet everything he was charged with involved only words: phone calls, letters—all oral and written words. Nobody in his right mind would suggest a First Amendment defense for what Wachtler did or that there is a First Amendment right to that kind of conduct. So the issue really turns out to be where and what kinds of words are protected, and what kind rise to the level of harassment, intimidation, threats, which are otherwise actionable.

Every city in this country prohibits harassment; nobody defines it with any precision. It plays itself out in the case law, and every time a case is presented in a First Amendment context to a group like the ACLU, somebody has to sit down and decide whether this is something we think ought to be protected speech, or whether it rises to the level of harassment that is actionable even though words are used.

I find nothing in this debate that makes it new. The issue that makes it new is a serious movement among some legal scholars to introduce more permissive First Amendment standards. The paradigmatic attempt is contained in the recent book by Mari Matsuda, Charles Lawrence, Richard Delgado, and Kimberlè Crenshaw called *Words That Wound*, in which they, as Catherine MacKinnon does in the area of sex and pornography, argue that certain kinds of speech, which up to now have been considered protected, ought to be punished because, in one way or another, they wound, or ought to be considered as torts. That is what is new about this debate.

I reject this argument out of hand, not only because it raises enormous threats to First Amendment rights for all of us, but because it especially threatens the very people that it is meant to protect.

Minorities are, by definition, normally not in a position of power. And if you aren't in power, then the standard advocated by Matsuda et al. is not one that you would like your enemies to apply to you. The key questions when evaluating the likely impact of any proposed speech restrictions are: Who enforces it? Who interprets what it means? Who selects its targets? Minorities have special reason to fear that those in power—who cannot be relied upon to be responsive to minorities—will most often use their discretion to limit the speech of minorities.

It is therefore not only for all the usual doctrinal reasons that I fear the elasticity of this new movement to widen the permissiveness of speech restrictions, but also because it's a political and strategic trap of the worst kind for the very people it is meant to benefit.

Consider the plight of minorities on a campus where they are grossly outnumbered, where the administration is mostly white, where it is responsive to alumni and funders who are mostly white, where people like Mari Matsuda and Chuck Lawrence argue, in effect, that minorities are an isolated, subjugated, subordinated, marginalized group in a larger majoritarian, oppressive, insensitive community. Is that the community minorities should want to endow with the discretion to limit speech?

If the speech codes that I have seen on college campuses around this country had been in force in the early 1960s, Malcolm X would have been their most frequent victim.

There is no doubt in my mind that when Rudolph Giuliani says that Louis Farakkhan should not be allowed to rent Yankee Stadium on the same basis as everyone else because of the content of his views, that is exactly what college campus after college campus would have said about Malcolm X and Eldridge Cleaver and almost anyone else who was on the cutting edge of justice rhetoric, much of which was antiwhite.

Consider that in the year that the University of Michigan speech code prevailed, before it was struck down in court, there were about twenty instances where whites charged blacks with violations, even though the purpose of the code was to protect and "empower" blacks. To my knowledge, there was not a single instance of a white student making antiblack comments who was punished. One black student was punished, however, for using the term "white trash." Is that what the advocates of speech restrictions had in mind? Consider that in the much-heralded MacKinnon-type statute on obscenity and pornography in Canada, the very first target of that law was a gay and lesbian bookshop. Consider that bell hooks, the black feminist author, had her book confiscated under that law by Canadian authorities.

Consider that in England in the 1970s when students, including Jewish students, succeeded in supporting and passing an ordinance that barred racist speakers from their campuses, those Jewish students were not happy when some years later that ban was applied to Zionist speakers on the grounds that somebody in power with the discretion to do so had decided that Zionism was a form of racism. The people who had supported that law lived to regret it.

People who are not in power have no stake in giving discretion over speech to people who are in power, particularly when they claim that the reason such discretion is needed is because the people in power are not sensitive to them and indeed are oppressive. It is strategically unintelligent and even politically conservative to support speech restrictions in that context. It is like using poison gas—it seems like a powerful weapon to use against your enemy, but the other side blows it back on you and they have stronger and more powerful fans.

The debate over speech restrictions troubles me most of all because I see it as a diversion from the underlying problem of persistent prejudice and bigotry. We are in this debate because certain people have defined it in a way that suggests that speech and equality are antagonists, when in fact freedom of speech has often been the precondition of movements for equality. If you allow the antagonistic definition of the speech-equality debate to prevail, then what will develop out of it will be destructive to both rights.

Turning the debate away from racial equality to focus upon the First Amendment as an imagined obstacle is, in fact, a terrible diversion. I sometimes think that if it were a Cointelpro operation it would not surprise me. It is a diversion. Why are we spending all of this energy on college campuses talking about some adolescent who says "water buffalo"? I do not mean to trivialize the insult of racist speech. If I could press a button tomorrow and get rid of it I would, but I would say that about a lot of political speech the First Amendment protects.

Why are we spending all that time on such incidents and not spending equivalent time addressing our underlying racial problems? On college campuses today you have kids who were five years old when Ronald Reagan took office. They have grown to political consciousness during a time when it became fashionable to suggest that the civil rights movement was over, that the problem of race was remedied, that affirmative action was reverse discrimination, that if you were black and not making it, it was your own fault. That's all they've heard. They've heard it from the president, they've probably heard it from their governor and mayor, and God knows what they've heard in their homes. These are the kids who are now on campus. They come there unlearned and insensitive. They come there thinking that black students are there because of affirmative action and not because of merit. They come there resentful, they come there full of prejudices. Black students come with their own baggage, their own racial scars. Often they come from segregated communities as well. And we put them together in the same dormitory. We provide little, if any, assistance. We ask them to share rooms and bathrooms and social settings, and then we wonder why, in moments of anger, they yell at each other with racial epithets. Then we pretend that the way that you cure the problem is to outlaw the epithets.

I think it is ridiculous. It is not only a First Amendment violation, but it is a disservice to the cause of equality, not to mention an abandonment of the obligation to educate. We are, after all, talking about *schools*.

My colleague Bill Rubenstein, who was the head of the ACLU's Lesbian and Gay Rights Project, makes an interesting point about the relationship between speech and equality. He says that the First Amendment has done more for gay rights than the Fourteenth Amendment—that the First Amendment is *about* being able to speak, that it is *about* being able to say who you are. What is the debate about gay rights in the military except the right to be open and not be punished for it? It is the First Amendment that has gained rights for subjugated groups. It is often the First Amendment that begins the attempt to apply the Fourteenth Amendment. The first fight for equality is often the fight for an equal right to *speech*. That is what drove the civil rights movement in the 1950s and 1960s in the South, what drove the prisoners' rights movement, what drove the mental patients' rights movement. It's what drives the gay rights movement today. Speech is often the first equality issue that you win. It is also often the predicate to a political movement that gains the rest. And in the area of gay rights, it is the substance of equality to a large extent. It is therefore a fundamental error, analytically as well as politically and strategically, to think of speech and equality as exclusive spheres. They are bound together in a way that is so integral that if we ignore the integration of those two rights, we disserve both. We cannot pretend that you gain one at the expense of the other or else we will reduce the vitality of both.

■ Martin Redish

In discussing the constitutionality of hate speech regulations, we should begin by drawing a very important distinction between first-party hate speech and third-party hate speech. Hate speech that is said directly in a coercive manner to someone who is an unwilling listener is not constitutionally protected. No one suggests, for example, that stalkers or those engaging in coercive or threatening kinds of speech are constitutionally protected. The idea of coercive free speech is an oxymoron. On the other hand, third-party hate speech is speech not said to an unwilling or unreceptive listener, but rather to presumably willing or at least neutral listeners about someone else. And it is in this situation that very serious constitutional problems are caused by government regulation.

Those in favor of hate speech regulations have sought to establish a tension between the First Amendment right of free speech and the Fourteenth Amendment right of equality. As a strategic matter, I suppose this effort makes perfect sense. If one is seeking to overcome a constitutionally based interest with a subconstitutional or nonconstitutional competing interest, one will usually lose. This strategy adopts the position of those who support hate speech regulation that there are competing constitutional interests, and at the very least, the constitutional interest in free speech is stalemated out of the picture. However, this is a totally false dichotomy on any level, whether doctrinal, textual, or theoretical.

First of all, the Fourteenth Amendment by its terms is limited to state action. This is not a trivial or technical kind of limitation. People can debate how far the concept of the state extends, and I think the current Supreme Court has been much too grudging in its definitions, but there can be no doubt that at some point in our society the individual must be viewed as separate from the state. And the individual is not controlled by the equal protection clause. If we were talking about hate speech limitations on government officials—for example, whether it would be a violation of the equal protection clause for a governor to have a Confederate flag—the state action issue can be debated; those are different questions.

When we're talking about a private individual, however, on both textual and historical levels, there exists no conflict at all. More importantly, the absence of any conflict can be seen by asking whether the First Amendment would protect a person's right to advocate repeal of the Fourteenth Amendment. Could anyone doubt that such expression is protected by the First Amendment? I think not. Yet in a very concrete sense, if such expression is persuasive and effective, it clearly undermines the Fourteenth Amendment.

The First Amendment must protect such advocacy, because as Peter Westen told us a number of years ago, the concept of equality cannot be viewed in a vacuum. Equality imposed by a totalitarian society would be at best a very superficial kind of equality. The concept of equality, then, is an outgrowth of our commitment to a democratic system in which we believe in the integrity of the individual, the very same belief which has also led us to adopt the principle of self-determination. And the principle of free speech, as Alexander Meiklejohn told us many years ago, is in many ways a logical outgrowth of our commitment to democracy. Individuals in the voting booth are the ultimate governors; the people we elect are merely our agents. Therefore any speech and any opinion that could influence the actions of the electorate in the voting booth, as governors, is protected under the First Amendment so that the democratic process may function successfully.

To the extent a particular interest or value has been constitutionalized it has, to be sure, been insulated from simple majoritarian control, but not from supermajoritarian control. The Constitution can be amended. Hence, if the democratic process is to work, society must commit itself to a concept of equality of ideas, as well as an equality of individuals and an equality of races.

An equality of races, when viewed apart from commitment to an equality of ideas and to self-determination in a democratic system, is basically a hollow form of equality. One might argue that such reasoning leads to a democratic paradox. The argument that equality is central to the democratic system, and that therefore the democratic system should not allow us to undermine equality, is similar to the flawed argument made in the early 1950s to justify restrictions on the expression of communists: They are seeking to destroy our democratic system; therefore we logically don't have to protect their speech. This is the paradox of democracy. Ironically, in trying to restrict the views of those who would undermine democracy, we are ourselves undermining the democratic system.

The defenses of regulation of so-called third-party hate speech are many, but none of them is ultimately persuasive. One is the argument that hate speech silences those about whom it is being said, and thus effectively undermines the free speech rights of those who have been silenced. In some ways that may be empirically true. But once you establish as a basis for drawing an exception to the First Amendment the concept that speech that indirectly silences someone else can be restricted, you have effectively gutted the First Amendment. For example, many feminist groups could be restricted on that ground because many people feel intimidated by them.

It has also been argued that hate speech may be regulated because it gives rise to emotional distress in the subjects of that speech. But consider a hypothetical statute, one that is surely not inconceivable in many state legislatures, providing that "whereas the view that a fetus is not a life causes serious emotional distress to numerous right-thinking individuals, it shall now be a crime to suggest that a fetus is not alive." Few could deny the empirical fact that numerous people who feel strongly about the issue of abortion are emotionally distressed by speech suggesting that a fetus is not a life, just as many people are emotionally hurt by the sight of the burning of the American flag. The First Amendment simply cannot allow that kind of private veto. The fact that one is emotionally hurt by speech is appropriately viewed as one of the necessary costs of the democratic process.

Finally, I want to talk about the issue that was involved in the *Mitchell* case, in which I wrote an amicus brief last year. People that I normally thought would line up on the side of free speech were on the other side on the question of regulating hate motivation. These laws enhance criminal sentences: If you commit a crime you go to jail for x number of years, but if it is found that you committed the crime because of the victim's race, then you go to jail for x plus two years or x plus three years.

Obviously, speech is not involved in the direct sense of the term here. No one would suggest that a political motivation for a violent act somehow insulates that act from regulation or punishment. But these enhancement laws do not regulate or punish the actual violent act. That is already punished by the laws prohibiting the criminal conduct itself. The only activity these laws punish is the underlying political or ideological thought or motivation that lies behind the criminal act.

That such laws give rise to serious First Amendment problems can be seen by examining the situation involved in *United States v. O'Brien*, the draft card burning case, in which the Supreme Court upheld, against First Amendment attack, a federal law making criminal the destruction of one's draft card. Imagine, however, that Congress had added to that act Section 2, saying, "Anyone who burns his draft card and is motivated in doing so by disagreement with United States policies in Vietnam will get an extra two years in jail." No protected speech was involved, yet I cannot imagine that any constitutional scholar would suggest that that hypothetical statute is constitutional. It seems to me that the First Amendment applies just as forcefully to racially based action as it does to ideologically or politically based motivation.

On a personal note, when I talk about this subject, it's often been said to me, "You're not African American, you're not female; how could you know what being the subject of hate speech feels like?" Obviously I'm not either of those things, but I am Jewish, and I have many relatives whom I will never meet because they died in Nazi death camps. There are very few things that I find as personally offensive as the sign of the swastika. Yet, I have no doubt that on a constitutional level, there is a First Amendment right to display the swastika anywhere in public because as much as I detest racial and religious bigotry, I fear much more any attempt by government to control the minds of its citizens.

■ Randall Kennedy

When Ira Glasser spoke of campuses, he did not distinguish among the sorts of campuses that we have in the United States. There are all sorts of campuses: Notre Dame and Yeshiva are religious schools; there are large public universities; there are large private universities; there are small private universities. So, the notion of "the Campus" is a complicated one. I come from a private university, and the point that I would like to focus on has to do with the question of the private university, not the public university.

With respect to public universities, I agree with what Glasser has to say, and in general I'd agree with what he had to say with regard to the politics of the matter, even with respect to private universities. But there is this one remaining issue where I think that some civil libertarians, and particularly that great champion of civil liberties, the American Civil Liberties Union, have gone wrong. And that is when the American Civil Liberties Union, and other champions of civil liberties as well, want to totally erase the distinction between public campuses and private campuses.

Now, one of the chief banners of the ACLU and like-minded champions of civil liberties is more speech. If you have a problem with what someone or some organization is saying, meet them with more speech. I can imagine a group of people who would take that to heart and who would say there is entirely too much cursing in the world, there is entirely too much use of racial epithets of various sorts, and so we want to create a campus that's going to be called the Clean Speech Campus—no cursing, no racial epithets, and everybody is going to be called and addressed by their last name. Mr. or Ms. Now, that's a point of view. I probably wouldn't want to go to that college or university, but the question is, Should we have a social/political/legal system that enables such a regime to exist? And it seems to me that we should, in the name of pluralism. More speech. Let a thousand flowers bloom.

Instead, we have on the part of civil libertarians an impulse to centralization, compulsion, and coercion. For example, the American Civil Liberties Union entered into a compact with, among others, Henry Hyde of Illinois to have Congress pass a statute that would essentially compel universities nationwide to conduct their business according to the dictates of what the Supreme Court says the First Amendment requires.

It seems to me that sort of compulsion is a bad thing. It represents the imposition of a particular ideology regarding freedom of expression, regarding the way in which academic institutions should comport themselves. Civil libertarians have been very concerned about the control of public money to regulate artists. They have been very concerned about the use of public money to regulate reproductive freedom. It seems to me that civil libertarians should be very concerned about the use of public money to regulate the way in which private parties want to construct various sorts of academic institutions. That, it seems to me, is a concern that Glasser and his other civil libertarian colleagues—which means all of us—need to address.

■ Discussion

JUDITH RESNIK: It may be helpful to put on the table the Stanford Code, which starts out by saying it is "committed to the principle of free inquiry and free expression." A paragraph of explanation follows, then it says, "intimidation of students by other students in their exercise of this right, by violence, threat of violence is therefore considered a violation." In the second paragraph, "Stanford is also committed to principles of equal opportunity and non-discrimination." It goes on to say, "Harassment of students on the basis of any characteristics such as sex, race, color, handicap, religion, sexual orientation, or national and ethnic origin contributes to a hostile environment that makes access to education for those subjected to it less than equal." The final paragraph states, "Speech or other expression constitutes such harassment by personal vilification if it (a) is intended to insult or stigmatize an individual or a small number of individuals on the basis of their sex, race, color, handicap, religion, sexual orientation, or national and ethnic origin and (b) is addressed directly to those individuals or individuals whom it insults or stigmatizes and (c) makes use of insulting or fighting words or nonverbal symbols."

It might be helpful to find out how these examples play out under Ira Glasser's rubric.

IRA GLASSER: To Randall Kennedy's point first, I was interested that you said at the beginning that you didn't have any quarrel or disagreement with my political analysis even on private campuses. So what you were making was really a legal point about state action and whether or not, as a constitutional matter, the government ought to be allowed to intrude those sorts of standards on private campuses.

RANDALL KENNEDY: That's largely true, but I don't want to trivialize it and say that it's merely a legalistic matter, because in the same way that I think that some of the people you were criticizing have generated a backlash and don't do any good for their side, I would similarly say that it's possible for civil libertarians to engage in a political initiative that's also counterproductive. The ACLU's position on this has made me rethink anew the public-private distinction and made me far more attentive and solicitous of private institutions than I would otherwise have been.

GLASSER: First of all, I entered this debate primarily as someone concerned with the persistence of discrimination, bigotry, and prejudice. That concern is no less focused upon private universities than public, and even if I agreed that the law ought not be able to intrude, all of the arguments I would make as a matter of policy against these kinds of codes would remain.

Second, the notion that you can relieve the sense of helplessness and somehow empower people by these codes, instead of focusing on relieving the helplessness itself, is a kind of a legal therapy that is more illusory than real. I have sat in too many university presidents' offices, behind closed doors— including a number of major universities—and had them tell me, "Well, you're right. But we had to give the black students a bone." They have literally said that. Others have been less crude and said, "We had to make a gesture." They all understand that this is a way of buying off a problem, and they're not anxious to get into the hard guts of the problem itself. In that sense, I think it disserves the equality principle to have these codes, even if it's just a matter of public policy.

On the legal matter, which I agree has a lot of consequences, it worries me that it causes you to rethink your position. I passed that point a long time ago when I considered and rejected all the arguments they made in the South about why a public accommodations statute should not apply to universities, to restaurants, to hotels, and why the civil rights employment discrimination laws should not apply to private employers. They made all of those arguments. The question that I'm left with is, If it's alright to take constitutional values and apply them by statute to the private sector for Fourteenth Amendment rights, why isn't alright to do so for First Amendment rights? In fact, we already do it for a constitutional right that's a First Amendment right, because all those statutes prohibit religious discrimination. So, I don't understand, unless you're prepared to open up those questions—which I hope you aren't—I don't understand where the principled line gets drawn.

KENNEDY: The fact of the matter is that the Civil Rights Act of 1964 is mainly premised on the Interstate Commerce Clause. Furthermore, with respect to the Civil Rights Act of 1964, Congress was somewhat attentive to associational and privacy freedoms. There is, for instance, with respect to public accommodations, an exception for private clubs. With respect to employment, there is an exception for employers employing less than fifteen people. But, beyond all of that, there is still the point I put to you, and you can't answer me with an analogy.

If a group of people want to get together and say, "We're tired of people going on campus and saying all sorts of things which in our view degrade a community of scholars. We don't think it's good for scholarship for people to go around using the word 'nigger' or the word 'kike.' If you're on this campus, you use that word and you're off it. We don't want that." Why isn't it consonant with your principles to let a thousand flowers bloom, and for those people to be able to speak by creating a campus that is to their liking? There are a lot of other campuses.

MARTIN REDISH: I really don't think you're being responsive because you're proving more than you want to prove. Everything you're saying could just as easily justify a racially segregated private university. To say that the 1964 Civil Rights Act was enacted under the Commerce power is totally unresponsive. You're not questioning the lack of federal power to pass this statute. You're questioning whether in exercising whatever federal power they're exercising, they are invading some pluralistic enclaves. The same could be said of the 1964 Civil Rights Act, and the fact of it's coming under the Commerce Clause doesn't in any way say that it's not violating some separate enclave. So, are you saying that same principle of pluralism should allow people to be at a racially segregated university?

KENNEDY: I would then respond that access to education is a very different kettle of fish. With respect to the employment market, it's one thing to exclude people, but the question is, Can one have a university setting where people are allowed to create the setting they want to have?

RESNIK: It may be helpful to focus on the fact that university settings are indeed a lot like that. Of course, there are norms that inform my classroom, and students are constrained in many ways in the kind and nature of the speech they engage in without invoking the First Amendment.

I think about how much I learn when people say to me that pornography is sufficiently painful that the citadel of the First Amendment should shake a little bit. Or that words can wound sufficiently that some of our First Amendment concepts need to be reframed. What that tells me is that there is something very serious at work here. Stanford's code is typically criticized as being unduly narrow, that it has responded to the "Michigan problem"—the University of Michigan code that was struck down because it went so far over that it was merely symbolic. By the way, many of us went to universities where people weren't supposed to say certain things in an era where your clean university didn't seem all that different from my private women's college, in terms of what was considered appropriate speech at the time.

There's a way in which your line, Ira, that "this is just like all the rest of the conflicts the civil liberties people have faced" is appealing. But then there's also a way in which it might be trivializing, because it turns out if you line a lot of these conflicts up, women of color, white women, men of color, people at certain class positions are repeatedly in these areas and examples.

GLASSER: I guess what I'm trying to say, Judy, is that I found Mari Matsuda's law review article, the first one she wrote trying to justify torts for speech, enormously moving and educating in the stories that she told and sensitizing to me, beyond what I thought was any longer possible. The point at which we part is whether or not because of those stories there ought to be codes that punish this speech.

Stanford is the best example for people who don't agree with me to throw at me because it's the narrowest and the closest and the only one I've seen in the whole country which even arguably avoids some of the problems. But I don't think it does and I'll say why.

First of all, if in order to pass constitutional muster—assuming that it was a state university where you had state action—even if it arguably does not violate the First Amendment, in order to avoid violating the First Amendment it is framed so narrowly that it avoids most of the speech that is the subject of the narratives. It grasps about 2 percent of what I would regard as bigoted, prejudicial speech that is the content of why most people are complaining about this. So, it doesn't even restrict most of what it is you want to restrict.

Part of my criticism is that we're spending a lot of energy playing out in the remote fields of this problem. My second criticism is that bigoted speech is only one part of bigotry. Discriminatory speech is only one kind of discrimination, and it is arguably not the worst kind. What about employment? What about housing? What about curriculum? What about affirmative action, both in student recruitment and faculty?

This debate is not about Stanford's code, it is about whether or not this is what should be consuming the argument about equality. I go on college campuses all the time. Not Stanford, but many of them tell me they can't get black students because they don't have enough black professors, and they can't get any black professors because there are hardly enough black Ph.D.s produced. When I ask them why that is so, and what they are doing about it, and what they are teaching about it to this group of kids who were five years old when Ronald Reagan took office, whether they have a course in the history of race in this country, most of them tell me no.

When you talk to kids about affirmative action one of the reasons they are hostile to it is because they don't understand it and because there's a discontinuity between their history and ours. One of the reasons you have so few black Ph.D.s is because of what's going on in the inner cities of this country, where homicide is the major cause of death for black males between the ages of eighteen and twenty-five and where 25 percent of the black males between eighteen and twenty-five who are not killed are under the jurisdiction of the criminal justice system. Where there are more black males in prison than in college. Why aren't they addressing those problems? They're schools—they ought to be teaching, but they don't. What they do is pass codes that ignore most of the other problems and even ignore most of the problems of bigoted speech.

The Stanford Code itself, when you really get down to defining harassment, says, "Speech that is intended to insult or stigmatize." I don't want that power in the hands of most university faculty. I don't want that power in the hands of Rudy Giuliani if he ever becomes a university president. I don't want it in the hands of John Silber. When Randy Kennedy wants to know why I'm so concerned about the speech of students on private campuses, it's because twenty years ago I was trying to figure out ways to defend kids who were being expelled from private colleges and high schools because somebody in charge didn't like their views on race or on the war in Vietnam or on gay rights. That's why.

KENNEDY: Your comeback at me about the civil rights laws was good, and you raise tough issues. The line-drawing problem makes me think that there are difficulties. Are there similar difficulties on your end? Let's imagine the people who want to have a small Marxist university and what they want to do is have only certain people at their university to inculcate a certain belief structure.

Are we a big enough and pluralistic enough country to allow that? Now, I agree that on the questions that you two put to me, it does pose a problem. If New York University, for instance, was to buy all of Manhattan south of Fourteenth Street things would get complicated. At what point does a university become large enough so that in certain ways it's no longer deemed to be private? But, let me throw the ball back at you. What about my private Marxist university that wants to create a certain belief structure and doesn't want William F. Buckley on campus?

GLASSER: It's the difference between a large apartment building and renting out a room in your own house for housing discrimination; the difference between a couple owning a mom-and-pop grocery store employing one clerk and Exxon. Those kinds of differences in the employment context can be extended to size in the context of speech. But it certainly has to be true that places like Harvard and Columbia and NYU have more in common with large state universities than they have with that small model.

KENNEDY: There are hundreds of universities. Okay, let's scale it down then, let's not talk about the universities you've named, which are very large places. Let's talk about a smaller university, like many thousands, hundreds of thousands of Americans go to.

REDISH: Hopefully you couldn't use the same principle to justify Ku Klux Klan U., a small private grouping of people who for, whatever misguided reasons, don't like people of other races or other religions and want to exclude them. To be consistent, one would have to say either pluralism and associational freedom applies or that these interests can be overcome by the legislative application of constitutional principles to private universities.

ALAN SUSSMAN: A few years ago, I defended a student at a small private university, Bard College, who had violated the speech code by saying some ugly words about a woman who happened to be his ex-girlfriend. Perhaps what isn't recognized is that once you're in this milieu of absolutely right and wrong, academics have very little patience with due process. Once you're in front of these student-faculty committees, due process really goes out the window. There just isn't any.

At this particular hearing, the press was excluded. The student had been kicked off campus a few days earlier and was not allowed to get back onto campus to gather witnesses in his own defense. When I met the witnesses for the first time, I was unable to speak with them because it was thought that I would tell them what to say. There was certainly no Fifth Amendment protection. There was no respect paid to due process whatsoever.

RESNIK: As someone who teaches about due process, I might point out that in many criminal proceedings one does not have the right to interview the opponent's witnesses in advance of the trial. Alan was obviously troubled by both the process of decision-making and its outcome. Could you imagine fairer processes and a better regime of rules about inappropriate address?

REDISH: The focus of our discussion has been on the issue of the private/public distinction. This at least implicitly acknowledges that when the state is involved, the regulation of third-party hate speech does violate the First Amendment. If that is implicitly being acknowledged, I consider that a major victory.

KENNEDY: I largely agree with what you said, but one thing really got to me: When you ended your piece you talked about having your loved ones perish in the holocaust, but that you support the right to show the swastika. Of course, there are a lot of democratic societies around the world in which Nazi parties are outlawed. Both Ira and Marty put a lot of faith on a prudential hypothesis. You both say, "Well, we've got to make sure that we've protected the rights of Nazis and the Klanspeople because who knows what's going to happen tomorrow." You have to say a little bit more for the person who says, "Well, what's going to happen is the Nazis and the Ku Klux Klan may get their rights upheld today, and then tomorrow, when it's the communists' and socialists' turn at bat, judges are going to find a way to squash them." It's an empirical judgment. Why do you have such faith that if you can establish these rights in a particular case, that precedent is going to have sufficient pull?

GLASSER: That's a very important question, particularly since I base most of my First Amendment analysis ultimately on strategic and political considerations. For me, the principle isn't the First Amendment, it's free speech, and the First Amendment is a strategy for protecting it. And it's a strategy which recognizes an uneven distribution of power which I find arrayed against me more often than not. So I figure I have a stake in getting as close to that neutral principle as I can.

Now you ask why, after all of history, I still have faith in that principle. It's because I don't give up too easily, and because I think that over my lifetime—and certainly over the lifetime of the ACLU—that principle has been expanded to protect more and more of the disfavored people in this society, and that it has been an instrument of gaining Fourteenth Amendment rights. Even if it's not perfect, I certainly don't want to become an accomplice to its not working, because what is the alternative? The alternative is I get to be vulnerable when I speak about all the causes I favor.

REDISH: I'm not quite as strategically based here. I'm thinking as an academic on a purely normative level, and I was only about four years old when the communists—and people who were even leaning somewhere in that ideological direction—were being suppressed. But I consider myself one of the modern descendants of those scholars who stood up then. And the simple answer is: you fight each battle as it comes.

RESNIK: One of the problems, Ira, with your Fourteenth Amendment-First Amendment move is that one of the reasons that the First Amendment is a vehicle for gay and lesbian rights is because the Court decided the Fourteenth Amendment wrong. It's not about the First Amendment, it's about the tragedy of the misuse of the Fourteenth Amendment.

You say, "I'm feeling pretty good; we're making some progress," but one of the ways one could hear the call for speech codes is that some people don't share your sense of progress, protection, and efficacy, and their claim for additional protection and their search for new remedies comes from a sense that, despite the effort to tell a more cheerful story, there's still a very deeply horrible story that they experience.

DAVID COLE: I find myself wanting to do what Norman Dorsen used to do, which is taking a position that I don't entirely agree with. I agree largely with the strategic and political points that Ira has made. But I don't agree with the political and strategic rhetorical device that Martin also used, which is that there isn't a conflict between equality and the First Amendment.

Someone said, "We can't pretend that we gain one at the expense of the other." We do in many contexts clearly gain one at the expense of the other. The freedom of employers, or co-employees, to speak freely denies equality to particular participants in the workplace. The ACLU recognizes that as a conflict and struggles with a way to resolve that conflict. But you don't resolve it by saying that conflict doesn't exist.

Ronald Dworkin recently wrote a piece in the *New York Review of Books* reviewing Catherine MacKinnon's book *Only Words*, in which he tries to make the same move. He says there's no real conflict between equality and liberty of speech because everyone ultimately has an equal right to speak and that's what it's all about. That is very neat doctrinally, but it doesn't recognize the fact that we don't live in a world which is neutral. It has the same problems that a formal equality perspective on the equal protection clause has, which is that if you apply formal equality principles to an unequal starting ground, you don't reach equality. Ira's points that strategically this is not a good way to move towards equality seem to me very good arguments. But people will stop listening if we don't concede at the outset that there is a very substantial conflict here.

GLASSER: I don't mean that there is no conflict, but that there is no zero-sum game. We're not sitting here with two values, equality and speech, occupying wholly distinct spheres that are in a fundamental way opposed to each other—that is totally false, analytically and empirically.

There clearly are conflicts on particular issues, mostly at the margins, and by saying margins I don't mean that these are unimportant issues. But they are not unique to this field. There are many constitutional rights which come into conflict with other rights, and when you're writing a brief, deciding a case, or taking a position, to choose one is to reject the other. But that's a very different thing from asking if we can have both equality and free speech. Not only *can* we have both, but you can't have one effectively without the other.

REDISH: Ira may agree with everything you said, David, but I sure don't. First of all, when I said the supposed conflict between the Fourteenth Amendment and the First Amendment is a false one, I didn't say there weren't competing interests. I said that to view them as competing *constitutional* interests of equal stature is false. Beyond that, I'm wondering how far one takes the principle David seems to be advocating. What about someone who says, "I think people of certain races are inherently inferior and therefore should be discriminated against, therefore should we repeal Title VII"? That speech, while it's tough to imagine it being done persuasively, could have a tremendous negative effect on equality. Once we've established the principle that harm to equality can justify restriction on speech, I don't see how you can avoid justifying restricting that speech. Yet, if you restrict that speech, there's effectively nothing left of the First Amendment.

To the extent that Title VII is punishing words that are more than words, they are actions, such as: "Unless you go to bed with me I am going to fire you." I have no problems with it. As Ira pointed out, Sol Wachtler didn't claim the First Amendment, even though he used words to commit crime. However, to the extent Title VII is used in the more remote hostile environment sense, without a first party direction, I think it is unconstitutional.

RESNIK: There's presumably no accident or coincidence that the Stanford Code uses the words "hostile environment," because that's the core of the concern.

DAVID RUDOVSKY: Where Martin Redish and Ira seem to differ is when we go from hate speech to hate crime. I agree with a lot of what was said about hate speech and the reasons why some of these codes cause a lot of problems. Hate crime presents a wholly different question. In a number of the antidiscrimination statutes, such as the housing statute, we say to someone, "You can be a bigot, you can say to yourself in your mind that I'd never want a black person to live in a room that I rent." We protect that. Not only do we protect that thought, we protect the right to say that. But when you become a landlord, we say it's a crime if you act on that belief. You can go to jail if you don't rent to a Jew or an Italian or a black person because of their race.

Hate crime is the same thing. If I assault you and I do it because you're black, I'm not being punished in that situation when the sentence is enhanced because I don't like black people, it's because I've *acted* on that belief. I picked you out simply because of some characteristic that we say can't be considered in that kind of act.

It's far different from burning a draft card and being punished because you did it because you're against the war effort. You can't be punished extra in this country because you commit a murder and they prove you're Republican. If your analogy is right, what do we do with all the antidiscrimination laws, which penalize, not only civilly but criminally, conduct based on motivation? Secondly, if you're right, what do we do in the entire sentencing process where we've always considered motivation as a factor, both mitigating and for harsher sentencing? Certainly, a judge can take into account that when you committed a particular crime, you did it with an invidious purpose.

Isn't the harm to the community when you select somebody because of race, or break that person's window, much more serious than a simple act of vandalism when the message you're sending to that person in the community is that you can't come here? Why can't the law address that factor?

REDISH: I see the antidiscrimination laws as distinguishable under the principle of *United States v. O'Brien*, the draft card burning case, when the Court held if what government is doing is punishing nonprotected conduct, the fact that incidental to that it sweeps within its punishment reach certain protected activities does not render the law unconstitutional.

You correctly pointed out that one may have a constitutional right to be a bigot, but it doesn't mean one has a constitutional right to act on it. When one discriminates on the basis of race, there is an element of underlying ideological-political-social thought that is getting punished. But it is only punished incidentally to the regulation of nonprotected conduct, the exclusion. Apply that in the context of the hate crimes situation. The nonprotected conduct is already being regulated in a way that the discriminatory conduct cannot be regulated apart from its discriminatory intent. When someone hits someone else, that person has committed a crime and is being punished for it. The addition of a punishment for an underlying racist social motivation is not essential to the achievement of the state's purpose of regulating the nonspeech conduct.

In terms of the argument that perhaps racial crimes cause greater harm than other kinds of crimes, if a statute is phrased in terms that have nothing to do with the underlying political or social motivation of the perpetrator of the crime but simply turn on what's done, I have no First Amendment problem with it. But if a statute says, "If you commit the same crime for which we have provided a two-year sentence against somebody of another race, regardless of the motivation, you will get four years," I see First Amendment problems with that.

As to what we've normally done in the sentencing process, while we've given judges wide discretion in picking sentences on the basis of a number of factors, one factor that a judge would not be allowed to take into account—at least openly—is that the individual was acting out of a motivation of being against the United States, or a pro-life or pro-choice concern. Even in the individualized sentencing process, I don't think we'd accept that.

Certainly motivation is often a factor used in criminal cases. What about the fellow who kills his uncle because he wants to inherit all his money, as opposed to a fellow who kills his uncle because his uncle is in terrible pain and is dying? Obviously a distinction would be drawn there. Where we don't accept a distinction, however, is on the basis of an underlying political, ideological, or social motivation, for two reasons: first, that is the motivation that is most subject to abuse; and second, given the underlying democratic groundings of the First Amendment, that is the kind of underlying thought that regulation would cause the greatest harm.

GLASSER: I think again this bias enhancement debate somehow always strikes me as a little bit beside the point. First of all, I don't think there's anything wrong with a society saying that there's a higher degree of vandalism involved if the person vandalized a house with the intent of driving someone out of the neighborhood on the basis of race, than if they just vandalized a house because it's a teenage prank.

I don't think that there's anything that offends the First Amendment if a society decides to make the intentional selection of victims based on race, gender, and religion a higher degree of assault, if you can prove it. On the other hand, if I vandalize a house and the inhabitants happen to be black and then they find out that I worked for David Duke the last time around, and try on that basis alone to charge me with a more serious crime, then that is unconstitutional—that is penalizing me for my views.

If I happen to write a letter to these people who just moved in as the first black family in the neighborhood, and I slip that letter under the door at night, and the letter says, "Nigger get out, or we'll burn your house down," that letter by itself—though it is full of words—is actionable. If I'm the one who burns the house down, and the letter is introduced as evidence of my intent, I think that kind of arson can be punished at a higher level than what I would call routine and petty arson or vandalism. The distinction comes about with the kind of evidence you can use: How contemporaneous is it? How remote is it? What does it involve? I would be very restrictive about that, and most bias enhancement laws would fall by our standards. But not all.

The real problem I have with bias enhancement laws is not a First Amendment problem. It is that I am nervous about giving more prosecutorial power to prosecutors when everything I know about the criminal justice system indicates disparities in how the criminal justice system works toward blacks. That is a different sort of concern, but the more important concern. Why in the world would I want to enhance prosecutorial power when at every stage in the criminal justice system, I find bias toward blacks in its implementation? Entering the debate that way, I think, is the way we should talk about it, and we never do because of this strange oppositional attitude we have about the First and Fourteenth Amendments, and the whole important discussion about whether we want bias enhancement laws from the standpoint of equality concerns never occurs.

QUESTION: We've talked about a hypothetical where one student makes racial epithets against another in the dormitory or on campus. What about in the classroom? What about a professor who insults in a racial way?

REDISH: It depends on how you are defining the word "insult." If by "insult" you mean in a one-on-one situation, referring to someone in a particularly negative, derogatory way, that could be deemed coercive, and I don't consider that protected by the First Amendment. However, in the context of a class setting, if a professor puts forward theories or views that are deemed to be offensive or insulting, I think protection of such expression is what the First Amendment's all about.

GLASSER: I agree that there is a difference, but it's a treacherous difference and you have to be careful how you define it. But there is a difference because power matters in the classroom as it does in the workplace. It even matters with some of the arguments we were having on private schools with Randy Kennedy, because how the school is organized to propagate a set of views, and its right to do so free of government interference, is a different question than how that school then treats a student who dissents in part from that ideology. Those differences are very important, but how you define them so people have academic freedom to espouse views as distinct from harassing and intimidating people over whom they have power is where I think the definitional work has to be done.

QUESTION: There might be another explanation for the constitutional legality of the enhanced bias crime. Take someone who engages in a holdup, one-on-one, contrasted with someone who engages in a holdup in which there are twenty people who are the targets of the holdup. Why can't the state take the position that the more people who are threatened or terrorized, the more serious is the crime?

The crime that has a biased, racial, or religious motive, is designed to victimize not only that particular target, but to terrorize an entire group. Doesn't that make it an enhanced threat to society and justify imposing a more severe sanction?

REDISH: The trouble with that argument is that the existing laws are simultaneously underinclusive and overinclusive to fit that goal. There would be no constitutional problem in allowing enhancement of a sentence when it is found that the crime was designed to terrorize a particular community. However, these laws aren't phrased that way. There are lots of groups and communities that can be terrorized for which there's not enhanced punishment. On the other hand, all these laws require is that there be an intent to do it against someone of another race, where there could have been no intent to terrorize. So, I would have no problem with a narrowly drawn law that was aimed at the specific concern.

92   Discussion

GLASSER: So you think it's possible to draft a bias enhancement law that does not offend the First Amendment?

REDISH: No, because the way I'm defining it, it wouldn't be a bias enhancement law. It would apply to cases where it is found that the intent and likely effect was to terrorize an identifiable group or community, such as the old Tylenol cases in Chicago.

QUESTION: I, too, was bothered by the ACLU's visible support for Representative Hyde's proposal, because the First Amendment was being used in effect to deny the First Amendment rights of private educational institutions, because it's my understanding that academic freedom is itself a First Amendment right, and the right of individuals to come together and associate to inculcate values is a First Amendment right. With Professor Kennedy, I believe that if a certain group want to associate for the purpose of inculcating certain values, that as a general proposition, that's protected by the First Amendment. What I see as the distinction between the Hyde statute prohibiting educational institutions from making the decision that equality considerations require some kind of speech codes and the civil rights laws is that the Supreme Court says there is no constitutional right to discriminate on the basis of race. But there is a constitutional right to associate for certain values.

REDISH: What if the values for which they want to associate are racist values?

QUESTION: There is no provision in the Constitution which allows an institution to discriminate on the basis of race, so there is no countervailing constitutional interest which can be weighed against the governmental interest. In the case of the Hyde law, we do have a countervailing constitutional interest, a countervailing constitutional right, and that's the constitutional right of the institution to academic freedom to come together and associate for particular values and purposes, and to inculcate those values and purposes.

GLASSER: But you misconstrue the Hyde bill. The Hyde bill says nothing at all about what the institution can say or espouse, or what a teacher can espouse. The Hyde bill is directed at the *student's* right to dissent from what the institution espouses. I find it a curious definition of academic freedom which says that the institution is protected in its academic freedom but the students who attend that institution are not. What I see is the kind of problem we had in New York twenty-five years ago when the United Federation of Teachers struck to have the right of due process before they were fired, and then resisted it when it was applied to student suspensions. The difference was who had power over whom.

KENNEDY: A case came up with respect to people wanting to parade. If people want to parade and express themselves, it might be a disgusting expression, but if they want to do that, sometimes exclusion is expressive. Now, if that's the case, why do you keep pressing me on white supremacist schools? The fact is that we have white supremacist schools. There are hundreds of white supremacist schools, private institutions around the country. Then you say, "But our law prohibits them from excluding students." That's true, and then I would be pressed to try draw a distinction between wholesale exclusion and merely propagating an idea. I still

94 Discussion

haven't gotten an answer from Ira Glasser on the question of why what I have said is inconsistent with pluralism. I'm taking the more speech banner from you. How do you get it back?

GLASSER: You have the answer, you just don't want to listen to it. I'll give it to you again. We're talking past each other on this because this Hyde law does not govern institutional speech, it governs the student's speech and what the institution can do.

RESNIK: A little false dichotomy here?

GLASSER: No, because what you're saying is that the institution's right to its speech is compromised if students at that institution disagree.

KENNEDY: Yes, that's right. If I have an institution and I want to inculcate a certain belief structure and this is my conception of the way in which people should think—it's just like when I run a class, by the way. People can't just get up and say whatever they want to say, whenever they want to say it. I'm running the class, I want to put forth a point of view.

GLASSER: Well, say I represent your students. You're talking to me about power. All you're saying is that you want the right to say everything in your classroom, and you want the right to punish people in your classroom who disagree.

SANDY WIDLAM: I find it frustrating that the whole issue of hate speech has been swept under the table, when people who come from groups that have been traditionally disempowered in our country because of sexism and racism truly do feel silenced when, based on those characteristics, they are cut down by speech.

What happens with hate speech is that before the speaker even has a chance to speak, he or she is considered inadequate either because of race or gender.

REDISH: I taught an undergraduate seminar on free speech theory three years ago, and when I reached the issue of pornography, there was a vigorous debate between me and a couple of feminist students about the role of First Amendment. And, after the class, totally independently of one another, five students came up to me and said, "Professor, I really agreed with you, I just don't feel comfortable talking in the class with those strident people making their points."

If you want to go down that path, if you want to start saying that "speech that silences justifies restriction of the speech," I think you're going to get results you don't like.

GLASSER: Taking racial justice for a moment, I believe that this country is in a deep state of denial about racism. I believe the word itself means something very different today from what it meant twenty-five years ago, and we don't even have the same definitions when we talk about it. I believe that state of denial is leaving deep and growing problems unaddressed in any serious way. I believe that as a legal community we are mired in the remedies of the past because the problems of the past were legal barriers, for which the remedies were lawsuits and new laws. And now, the problems are mostly socioeconomic and political disparities, and legal remedies don't work well for that.

Lawyers love to do what they do best, the same way as police chiefs and architects and surgeons. You go to a surgeon with a medical problem, he'll cut you. You go to a lawyer, and he'll draft a statute. But codes and legal remedies are not for the most part what the problem is about now, and to talk about seriously empowering disempowered minorities in this country at this time by passing codes that outlaw someone's saying "water buffalo" trivializes the problem of equality and how far we yet have to go. The First Amendment problems are easy. Let's stop talking about this, and let's get to the hard business of remedying continuing inequality.

RESNIK: With respect to Marty's comment about "stridency," some words do wound. We do not all start in the same place in this world, and our experience of speech may not be equal. A moment of silence for one person may be their first experience of silence in much of their life, where another individual may have felt constrained for a good part of their lives.

REDISH: I didn't use the word "strident," the students who came up to me used that word. The only point I was making was once you start by saying speech that intimidates or silences is a basis for restricting the speech, you've created a morass of empirical problems and invited abuse of that kind of standard.

KENNEDY: The seeming split, or bad feeling, or tension between the forces of civil libertarians, and the forces of racial and gender equality, is an issue that civil libertarians and all of us are going to have to pay more attention to. It's too bad that people often think of the struggle for black liberation, in particular, as being somehow apart from the

ACLU and other similar organizations when these organizations and people allied with them have carried on in such a passionate and strong way. When one thinks of Mississippi in the 1960s, one thinks of Eleanor Holmes Norton of the ACLU and others.

■ PART THREE

Workplace Harassment

■ Susan Deller Ross

For some years now, litigators, judges, and academics have been grappling with a number of controversial issues in sexual harassment law. Today's "sexy" controversy concerns the First Amendment and Title VII of the 1964 Civil Rights Act,[20] the federal law prohibiting gender discrimination in the workplace. Does Title VII go too far when it tells employers they may not create different working conditions for female employees than for male employees, if it is "verbal ... conduct of a sexual nature"[21] that creates the difference? All would concede there is discrimination if an employer assigns women and black men to small offices without air-conditioning, while giving white men large air-conditioned offices because of their gender and race. Even if the women and black men perform superbly in their small, hot offices—even if they do not suffer anxiety and debilitation from their unequal treatment, but are simply offended by it—most of us would think they are entitled to a court injunction stopping the differential treatment, and to some damages as compensation for the stigma of having to work in an inferior office.

But when different working conditions for women are created by an employer's speech—say, by regularly calling all female workers obscene names—the red flag goes up. This is pure speech, the argument goes, and it's being banned merely because it's offensive to women. Therefore, Title VII cannot reach such conduct, or it will violate the First Amendment. We must interpret Title VII to allow just a little bit of discrimination—the offensive sexual speech that demeans only women, making them feel unwelcome in the workplace. Never mind if some women quit their jobs because that's the only way they can avoid the verbal abuse. Never mind if other women don't apply to that employer because of its reputation for harassment. It's merely offensive speech and therefore must be protected, or the harassers' First Amendment rights will be infringed.

How did we get to this particular controversy? And is this the result the First Amendment requires us to reach? I think not. But before discussing the constitutional and policy considerations that lead me to that conclusion, I'd like to retrace the history of sexual harassment law, to put the matter in some perspective and to enable us to gauge the First Amendment argument more fairly and completely.

The current controversy may stem from the label "sexual harassment" itself. Early on, it served us well by giving a catchy title to a previously unnamed problem. It disserved us, however, when it turned our focus from the gender discrimination that Title VII forbids—treating female employees differently than male employees because of their sex—to the subject of sexuality. And, as always, sexuality was distracting. It made us think that we were dealing with sex with a capital "S," rather than different treatment because of one's gender. So it seemed to many that "sexual harassment" cases were just about stopping dirty jokes and expressions of sexuality in the workplace. But that's not what these cases are really about, as their history demonstrates.

The first question female workers faced in bringing this new kind of case was fairly simple, but illustrative of the core definitional problem: If a male supervisor asked a woman to have sex with him, was rejected, and retaliated by demoting or firing her, was that gender-based discrimination? Why no, said the lower federal courts. Such a situation merely reflected "an inharmonious personal relationship."[22] In other words, this was merely a social-sexual issue, one having nothing to do with gender discrimination in the workplace.

The federal circuit courts, however, soon began reversing these decisions.[23] Of course it was discrimination based on sex, they said. Only women lost their jobs for turning down sexual overtures; no men did. Notice that it was not the fact that *sexuality* was involved that made it sex discrimination. Rather, it was the fact that female subordinates were treated *differently* than male subordinates. This first kind of sexual harassment case soon became known as "quid pro quo" harassment, and employers and courts settled down to coping with it.

Other issues quickly followed, just as controversial in their turn. What if a woman didn't want to have sex with her boss but was too scared of losing her job to turn him down? If she had intercourse with him, and subsequently received good promotions and pay, did she have a Title VII claim? After all, she had lost no economic benefit; surely the sole injury of being coerced into unwanted sex wasn't enough to be covered by Title VII. When Michelle Vinson sued on these facts alleging sexual harassment, the Supreme Court spoke for the first time on the subject. Even Justice Rehnquist agreed, in *Meritor Savings Bank v. Vinson*,[24] that imposing coercive sexual intercourse upon women was illegal sex discrimination, since no men had to work under these conditions. And the Court approvingly quoted the Equal Employment Opportunity Commission (EEOC) guidelines that define this *second* kind of sexual harassment case—"hostile environment" harassment:

> Unwelcome sexual advances, requests for sexual favors, and other verbal or physical conduct of a sexual nature constitute sexual harassment when ... such conduct has the purpose or effect of unreasonably interfering with an individual's work performance *or* creating an *intimidating, hostile, or offensive working environment*.[25]

The Court added other requirements to the proof of such cases. Besides showing that the sexual conduct was based on gender—that is, applied only to workers of one sex—the plaintiff must show that the conduct was unwelcome, that she indicated this, and that it was severe or pervasive enough to change her working conditions.

Unfortunately, *Vinson* didn't put a stop to the controversy. The lower courts hated "hostile environment" cases. They feared the flaky, hypersensitive women who would build a federal case over nothing. Over mere words, for example. So the lower courts created new barriers in the law, ones not in existing sexual harassment law.

The Sixth Circuit took the lead, in *Rabidue v. Osceola Refining Co.*[26] Led by two Reagan appointees, the court came up with four new hurdles for sexual harassment plaintiffs. Under the new conservative standard, such women first had to prove they were psychologically injured by the harassment—a requirement not imposed by either the EEOC or the Supreme Court. Contorting the EEOC guidelines yet again, the judges also required plaintiffs to prove both that the harassment affected their job performance *and* that it created a hostile, offensive, or intimidating environment, rather than either one or the other, as the EEOC allowed. This new hurdle effectively eliminated the existing right to sue independently under either standard. Finally, the judges required, with regard to each of the new hurdles, that plaintiffs prove not only actual injury to themselves, but also that a hypothetical reasonable person would have suffered the same injury. The victim who could prove actual injury under the new tough test of psychological injury *plus* job performance effect *plus* offensive environment would still lose if the employer could convince the court that reasonable victims would not be so injured.

Now how did the Sixth Circuit measure how "reasonable people" would be affected? Why, it was easy. They examined their own subjective, gut feelings about the facts. So when Rabidue and other women objected to being called "whore," "cunt," "pussy," and "tits" on the job, in an environment where no men were called sexually demeaning names, the judges knew how reasonable people would react. Reasonable people would not be psychologically injured, their job performance would not suffer, and they certainly wouldn't find the work environment created by the verbal conduct to be intimidating, hostile, or offensive but merely "annoying." After all, the Sixth Circuit reasoned, "[I]n some work environments, humor and language are rough hewn and vulgar. Sexual jokes, sexual conversations and girlie magazines may abound. Title VII was not meant to—or can—change this. . . . Title VII was [not] designed to bring about a magical transformation in the social mores of American workers."[27] So what if women are called obscene names as a condition of employment, while men are called Mr. Krupansky or Mr. Milburn (the two judges in the *Rabidue* majority)? That's not serious sex discrimination. That's just the way life is—as any reasonable person knows.

Rabidue led inexorably to another Sixth Circuit decision, one just as hostile to the idea of equal dignity on the job for women workers. This case concerned Teresa Harris, a woman manager who was harassed by the president (Charles Hardy) of the equipment rental company where she worked. As with Vivienne Rabidue, the trial court found her merely a victim of comments that "cannot be characterized as much more than annoying or insensitive,"[28] whether judged from the perspective of the reasonable person or the reasonable woman.[29] This court did find, however, that some of Mr. Hardy's remarks were offensive and one was "truly gross and offensive," both to Ms. Harris and to a reasonable woman manager.[30] So what were these "annoying" comments that Charles Hardy made only to women? Teresa Harris's lawyers informed the Supreme Court that:

(a) Mr. Hardy stated to Ms. Harris in the presence of other employees at Forklift [the equipment rental company], "You're a woman, what do you know," on a number of occasions and also stated, "You're a dumb-ass woman." . . .

(b) Mr. Hardy, on a number of occasions, stated to Ms. Harris, in the presence of other employees of Forklift, "We need a man as the rental manager."

(c) Mr. Hardy, in front of a group of other employees and a customer of Forklift, stated to plaintiff, "Let's go to the Holiday Inn to negotiate your raise."

(d) Mr. Hardy asked Ms. Harris and other female employees, but not male employees of Forklift, to retrieve coins from his front pants pocket. As Ms. Harris testified: "He would say, Teresa, I have a quarter way down there. Would you get that out of my [front] pocket."

(e) Mr. Hardy threw objects on the ground in front of Ms. Harris and other female employees of Forklift, but not male employees, and asked them to pick the objects up, thereafter making comments suggesting how they should dress to expose their breasts.

(f) Mr. Hardy told female employees that he had heard that eating corn would make their breasts grow.

(g) Mr. Hardy commented with sexual innuendos about clothing worn by Ms. Harris and other female employees of Forklift but not male employees.

(h) Mr. Hardy told Ms. Harris on a number of occasions that she had a "racehorse ass," and said that she could not wear a bikini "because your ass is so big, if you did there would be an eclipse and nobody could get any sun."

(i) Mr. Hardy suggested that he and Ms. Harris should start "screwing around."[31]

When Teresa Harris confronted her boss, he promised to stop. But shortly thereafter, he suggested in front of fellow employees that she had promised sexual favors to a customer in order to win an account for Forklift Systems. Or as Hardy put it, "What did you do, Teresa, promise the guy at ASI bugger Saturday night?"[32]

Using the new, tough *Rabidue* hurdles, the federal magistrate, district court judge, and appellate panel all found it easy to reject Teresa Harris's claim. They acknowledged that she proved that Hardy inflicted this treatment only on female employees. They found that it offended her, and would have offended the reasonable woman, and even that it continued after she explicitly told her boss it was unwelcome. The judges also agreed that the verbal conduct constituted a pattern of demeaning treatment toward women and that most of it was sexual in content. But, they decided, the controlling points against her were that it didn't psychologically injure or affect the job performance of either Harris *or* the hypothetical reasonable woman manager. So Harris lost before these judges.

Teresa Harris was undeterred, however, and took her case to the Supreme Court. There, although the Court took the case to decide only one issue, it ended up deciding three issues. The original issue was whether a plaintiff was always required to establish that she suffered psychological injury as a sine qua non of a successful lawsuit, as the lower court judges had ruled. But in an interesting about-face, Forklift abandoned its victory in the lower court on this point and advanced a slightly weaker version of the test, one it copied from two friend-of-the-court briefs that had already been submitted to the Court. Before the Supreme Court, the employer now claimed for the first time that a plaintiff could only establish sexual harassment by proving either psychological injury *or* an effect on her job performance—not both, as it had originally claimed in the lower courts. But this proposed standard would still have eliminated a plaintiff's then-existing right under *Vinson* and the EEOC guidelines to prove harassment by showing that the employer's conduct creates an "intimidating, hostile, or offensive" working environment, without regard to its effect on the woman's job performance or psychological state. Whether that existing right should be eliminated was thus the second issue in the case. The third issue was whether the conduct's impact on the actual victim was enough to establish a case. In other words, did she *also* have to prove the same impact on a reasonable victim, woman, or person?

How did the First Amendment come into this picture? The American Civil Liberties Union (ACLU), American Jewish

Congress (AJC), and Feminists for Free Expression (FFE) brought it there by arguing, in two friend-of-the-court briefs, that plaintiffs should *not* be able to sue solely under the "intimidating, hostile, or offensive" branch of the EEOC sexual harassment guideline, just as the conservative Sixth Circuit had effectively ruled in *Rabidue*. The ACLU, AJC, and FFE contended that this EEOC standard should be eliminated in order to preserve male workers' free speech rights. As the ACLU/AJC brief framed the issue: "It is essential ... that the effort to eradicate discrimination not ignore First Amendment rights or confuse nondiscrimination with political orthodoxy. We therefore disagree with the notion that 'offensiveness' is the touchstone of a Title VII violation."[33] Thus, these groups argued that women workers should be limited to suing over sexual harassment that met either the work performance or psychological injury tests, with the added protection for male workers of a "reasonableness" screen, and that women should *not* be able to sue over "intimidating, hostile, or offensive" sexual harassment.[34]

In a sure sign that this proposed cutback of women's rights generated intense controversy within the ACLU, its brief was signed only by two male lawyers, neither of them associated with the ACLU's Women's Rights Project. The Project had submitted briefs in every significant women's employment discrimination case to go before the Supreme Court since the early 1970s. Its failure to do so now was telling.

From a public policy perspective, the ACLU/AJC/FFE argument really didn't make sense. It required a woman to suffer harassment until the point that she was either psychologically injured or affected in her work performance, and until she could somehow prove that reasonable victims would also be so affected. Only then could she sue to stop the harassment. Under this theory, courts could not intervene to stop future serious harm from occurring while the present harm was more subtle. The courts would have to wait until the victims were in really bad shape, and the company owed them a lot of money for damages, before taking action.

Barring courts from taking effective preventive action against sex discrimination in the workplace couldn't be what Congress intended in enacting Title VII. Indeed, the strength of this public policy argument was undoubtedly the reason Forklift dropped its argument that all sexual harassment victims must always establish that they were psychologically injured in order to prevail. But Charles Hardy's lawyers saw that the ACLU/AJC/FFE position would accomplish the same goal, while sounding more respectable. So Hardy, too, proposed eliminating the "intimidating, hostile or offensive" branch of the EEOC standard, and likewise agreed with the ACLU, the AJC, and the FFE that successful cases should be limited to sexual harassment either causing psychological injury to the victim or affecting her job performance, with the added hurdle of the "reasonableness" screen to further protect the harassers. Forklift even emulated the concern expressed in the FFE brief that "merely offensive" speech should be allowed in the workplace. Indeed, the *grande finale* to Hardy's argument was that "the courts can avoid a direct conflict with the First Amendment only by ensuring that Title VII regulates employment practices and not, as [Harris] proposes, merely offensive speech."[35]

Is there a true First Amendment problem here? I don't think so, though the strategy of characterizing the issue as one of mere offensiveness was a clever one. What does this "merely offensive" formulation leave out?

To begin with, sexual harassment cases are not about sexual negotiations between equal social partners who are each free to walk away from the conversation. Women in the workplace are the quintessential "captive audience." They are usually the subordinates of the men who harass them. As the NAACP Legal Defense Fund and the National Council of Jewish Women told the Supreme Court in Harris's case: "Women and minorities often use the same word to describe individuals who confronted their bosses [over harassment] ... —unemployed."[36] Even when harassers are co-workers, women often can't escape having to work with the men who call them obscene names. Women who are forced to sue to stop the conduct have usually encountered men who refuse to stop, and managers who accept the behavior by allowing it to continue despite the victims' complaints. The only way a woman can escape such harassment is by quitting her job, an option most women workers cannot afford. Women's rights groups graphically made this point to the Court as they countered the Sixth Circuit's belief that the prevalence of "sexual jokes, sexual conversations and girlie magazines" renders them harmless in the workplace:

The ... suggestion that "erotica" pervades society misses an important distinction between society as a whole and a confined workplace. "Girlie" magazines are not generally displayed openly on newsstands, and no one is forced to purchase them. Television has a power switch, a tuner, dozens of channels from which to choose, and decency standards. Movies have ratings for sex, violence, and language. The common element is free choice—one is subjected to "erotica" only if one chooses to be. The workplace is another matter altogether. If pornography is displayed in areas that an employee must frequent incident to his or her job, he or she has lost the free choice to view such material or not. A woman who must choose between viewing lewd and demeaning pictures every day and quitting her job can hardly be said to have a "free" choice.[37]

The Supreme Court has repeatedly rejected First Amendment challenges to speech where the audience cannot choose to avoid the speech. *Frisby v. Schultz* is a recent example.[38] In 1988, the Court upheld a ban on picketing near residences, reasoning that "the resident is figuratively, and perhaps literally, trapped within the home, and . . . is left with no ready means of avoiding the unwanted speech."[39] The woman in a sexually harassing workplace is no less trapped.

While the woman is trapped, the harasser has plenty of other options for self-expression. His speech is not totally banned; he is just requested to express himself elsewhere, in another place—namely, not on the job site, but in a social setting or public fora where the recipient of his remarks is free to walk away if she chooses, without severe financial repercussions for doing so. Again, the Court has spoken approvingly of restrictions that effectively move speech to another location. In its 1986 decision in *Renton v. Playtime Theatres*, for example, the Court upheld an ordinance prohibiting adult theaters from locating within a thousand feet of any residential zone, family dwelling, church, park, or school. Quoting from an earlier case, the Court explained that it is the "secondary effect [of economic deterioration around adult theaters] which these zoning ordinances attempt to avoid, not the dissemination of 'offensive speech' "[40] and that if the city " 'had been concerned with restricting the message purveyed by adult theaters, it would have tried to close them or restrict their number rather than circumscribe their choice as to location.' "[41]

This point is even more telling when we realize that in sexual harassment cases it is not the harassing speaker who is usually asserting a right to speak, but his corporate employer. And the company does not do so to protect its own free speech rights as a business entity, or to advance any legitimate business interests, since the speech in question has nothing to do with the business. Rather, the company is simply trying to save money by avoiding Title VII liability for the individual, nonbusiness speech of its employees. Indeed, only the *defendant* employer has such an interest; employers not before a court would be better served by a clear-cut rule that says stop when you learn the verbal sexual conduct is discriminatorily directed toward one sex (usually women), is unwelcome, and is intimidating, hostile, or offensive to some or all of those women. That rule would stop the behavior and thus avoid future liability for employers. It would also ensure that all jobs are open to all workers without discrimination based on gender. No woman subject to verbal sexual harassment would feel forced to walk off the job to avoid the humiliation or to suffer it in silence rather than risk the consequences of speaking out. In short, the rule would prevent harassment from escalating to a really serious level, in contrast to the ACLU/AJC/FFE/employer's proposed limitation of harassment cases to those causing psychological injury or an effect on job performance, with the additional limitation of a "reasonableness" screen. That test insures that sexual harassment must escalate before it can be stopped.

Another point is that courts have frequently upheld different governmental restrictions on workplace conduct that involves speech because of the special nature of the workplace and the economic realities of employer-employee relationships. For example, one federal court of appeals ruled that public school teachers could be prohibited from holding faculty prayer meetings on school property because "the workplace is for working."[42] The Supreme Court has ruled that the National Labor Relations Act's ban on employer speech containing "a threat of reprisal or force or promise of benefit" did not violate the employer's free speech rights. Thus, a company president's antiunion speech predicting that unionization would result in a loss of jobs was not protected by the First Amendment. In reaching its decision, the Court considered the context of the "labor relations setting" and specifically the tendency of economically dependent employees to "pick up" the employer's "intended implications ... that might be more readily dismissed by a more disinterested ear."[43] Similarly, the Court upheld an application of the Railway Labor Act against a First Amendment challenge from nonunion employees who objected to contributing money to the union's social activities, publications, and conventions. The Court explained that

> by allowing the union shop at all, we have already countenanced a significant impingement on First Amendment rights. The dissenting employee is forced to support financially an organization with whose principles and demands he may disagree.... It has long been settled that such interference with First Amendment rights is justified by the governmental interests in industrial peace.[44]

When the governmental interest at stake is not just the maintenance of industrial peace, but rather ending this country's long history of egregious discrimination against women and blacks, the Court has explained in most emphatic terms that the government's compelling interest in preventing invidious discrimination may well take precedence over an assertion of First Amendment rights.[45] That interest becomes even stronger when a federal antidiscrimination law like Title VII is passed pursuant to congressional authority under Section 5 of the Fourteenth Amendment,[46] creating an explicit constitutional conflict between equal protection equality rights and free speech rights. Most advocates of First Amendment free speech rights for harassers have not recognized the existence of the countervailing and equally compelling Fourteenth Amendment equal protection rights of victims.[47]

Since Title VII and the multitude of state antidiscrimination laws were passed, however, a host of discriminators have learned this lesson the hard way. They found no solace at all in the First Amendment, though not for want of trying. In 1973, for example, the *Pittsburgh Press* sought refuge in the First Amendment's speech and press freedoms for its practice of publishing sex-segregated want-ad columns for employers. Interestingly, just as in Teresa Harris's case, the ACLU was torn apart by that first conflict between equality and free speech. One faction fought strenuously to file a Supreme Court brief that would give preference to the rights of the press to aid the discriminatory employers. The other faction, led by then-Professor Ruth Bader Ginsburg (now a justice on the Court), fought for a brief giving priority to women's equality on the job. You may not be too surprised to learn that her views prevailed, both within the ACLU and in the Court, where the newspaper's First Amendment argument was firmly rejected:

Any First Amendment interest which might be served by advertising an ordinary commercial proposal and which might arguably outweigh the governmental interest supporting the regulation is altogether absent when the commercial activity itself is illegal and the restriction on advertising is incidental to a valid limitation on economic activity.[48]

Similarly, a decade later, the Court rejected a law firm's argument that Title VII's application to partnership decisions that discriminated against women violated the male partners' First Amendment rights to free expression and association. As the Court noted, " 'Invidious private discrimination may be characterized as a form of exercising freedom of association protected by the First Amendment, but it has never been accorded affirmative constitutional protections.' "[49]

Clubs and other associations have also consistently failed in their First Amendment challenges to state antidiscrimination laws that barred them from excluding women from their membership rolls. The New York State Club Association, the Rotary International, and the Jaycees all learned in a series of cases in the mid-1980s that the Court would not use the First Amendment to rescue them from having to deal with women as co-equals.[50] Indeed, it was in the Jaycees' case that the Court so clearly preferred equality values over First Amendment values: "We are persuaded that Minnesota's compelling interest in eradicating discrimination against its female citizens justifies the impact that application of the [Minnesota human rights] statute to the Jaycees may have on the male members' associational freedoms."[51]

Even in a situation where the Court's ruling could have suggested a willingness to strike down sexual harassment law as unconstitutional, the Court was careful to point to the opposite conclusion. In 1992, the Court struck down the St. Paul, Minnesota, Bias-Motivated Crime Ordinance because it banned symbols—like burning crosses—that arouse race or gender-based anger in others, but did not prohibit other forms of "fighting words." Justice Scalia's opinion for the Court explained that the prohibition violated the First Amendment because it was not neutral in content as to all such speech. But he went on to propose a rationale for treating a ban on sex-discriminatory speech at work differently than the ban on public expression of hate speech. Prohibiting workplace discriminatory speech was part of a rule directed toward *conduct*, not speech, he said, and therefore did not violate the First Amendment:

[S]ince words can in some circumstances violate laws directed not against speech but against conduct (a law against treason, for example, is violated by telling the enemy the nation's defense secrets), a particular content-based subcategory of a proscribable class of speech can be swept up incidentally within the reach of a statute directed at conduct rather than speech. . . . Thus, for example, sexually derogatory "fighting words," among other words, may produce a violation of Title VII's general prohibition against sexual discrimination in employment practices.[52]

He then cited the EEOC guidelines on sexual harassment, making clear that he was specifically suggesting that these guidelines did not violate the First Amendment.[53]

So it was not a surprise when the Supreme Court reached a similar result in Teresa Harris's case, though it did so without explicitly discussing the First Amendment.[54] In November 1993, Justice Sandra Day O'Connor, writing for a unanimous Court, rejected the ACLU/AJC/FFE/employer's proposed test requiring a sexual harassment victim to prove either psychological injury to herself or an effect on her work performance in order to prevail in a sexual harassment case. As Justice O'Connor explained, "no single factor is required." Thus, it remains possible for women workers to sue to stop sexual harassment that creates an "intimidating, hostile, or offensive" working environment, despite the ACLU/AJC/FFE/ employer effort to eliminate women's remedy for this form of sexual harassment.

Moreover, this result occurred in a case involving "mere words." Charles Hardy never touched Teresa Harris. He simply denigrated her by verbally demeaning all women ("You're a woman, what do you know"; "We need a man as a rental manager"; "You're a dumb-ass woman") and by suggesting in front of others that she was a slutty sexual object ("Let's go to the Holiday Inn to negotiate your raise"; "Let's start screwing around"; "What did you do, Teresa, promise the guy . . . bugger Saturday night").

Finally, in an unusual twist, the employer in this case was the same person as the sexual harasser. Charles Hardy held both roles, and thus was that rare employer who really was asserting his own individual "free speech" right to talk abusively to women employees, rather than merely protecting his company's pocketbook by defending the offensive speech of other men who worked for him. Yet the Court did not even feel the need to discuss the First Amendment issue, though Charles Hardy, the ACLU, the American Jewish Congress, and Feminists for Free Speech had all clearly raised the issue in their briefs. Instead, Justice O'Connor's opinion and the concurring opinions of Justices Ginsburg and Scalia all saw the core issue in sexual harassment cases as *discrimination*—treating women differently than men.

Justice O'Connor started by quoting from the Court's first sexual harassment decision: " 'The phrase "terms, conditions, or privileges of employment" evinces a congressional intent to strike at the entire spectrum of *disparate treatment of men and women* in employment,' which includes requiring people to work in a *discriminatorily* hostile or abusive environment."[55] She concluded: "When the workplace is permeated with '*discriminatory* intimidation, ridicule, and insult,' ... that is 'sufficiently severe or pervasive to alter the conditions of the victim's employment and create an abusive working environment,' ... Title VII is violated."[56]

Justice Ginsburg agreed, as one might have anticipated: "The critical issue, Title VII's text indicates, is whether members of one sex are exposed to disadvantageous terms or conditions of employment to which members of the other sex are not exposed."[57] And so did Justice Scalia: "[T]he test is not whether work has been impaired, but whether working conditions have been *discriminatorily* altered." Thus, those who wanted to discard some equality rights in favor of expanding free speech rights did not succeed in convincing anyone on the Court that this case was about "merely offensive" words, rather than about Charles Hardy's discrimination in verbally denigrating a female worker but no male workers.

Teresa Harris's case is probably not the end of the discussion about whether Title VII, the EEOC guidelines, and court decisions in sexual harassment cases permissibly eradicate pervasive discrimination pursuant to the Fourteenth Amendment or instead impermissibly interfere with free speech in violation of the First Amendment. Justice O'Connor's opinion did contain one note of hope for those who would elevate free speech rights over equal protection rights, when she wrote that the Court's standard

takes a middle path between making actionable any conduct that is merely offensive and requiring the conduct to cause a tangible psychological injury. As we pointed out in *Meritor*, "mere utterance of an ... epithet which engenders offensive [sic] feelings in an employee" ... does not sufficiently affect the conditions of employment to implicate Title VII. Conduct that is not severe or pervasive enough to create an objectively hostile or abusive work environment—an environment that a reasonable person would find hostile or abusive—is beyond Title VII's purview. Likewise, if the victim does not subjectively perceive the environment to be abusive, the conduct has not actually altered the conditions of the victim's employment, and there is no Title VII violation.[58]

Thus, in a slight nod to free speech advocates, she acknowledged that "mere utterance" of a single epithet is not enough for a federal case. She also accepted the ACLU/AJC/FFE/employer test requiring the victim to prove that reasonable people (other than the victim) would be offended by the remarks in question.[59] Moreover, the Court did not agree to decide a First Amendment issue when it took the case, so it may be overly broad to read the case as a decision on the First Amendment issue first brought up by friends of the court and the employer at the later briefing stage.

The fact remains that the ACLU, AJC, FFE, and Charles Hardy squarely raised the First Amendment issue in their briefs, explicitly suggested getting rid of women's legal remedy for "intimidating, hostile, or offensive" sexual harassment in order to expand free speech rights, and lost that fight. Similarly, while the lone "mere utterance of an ... epithet" remains insufficient to prove a case, Teresa Harris won a ruling that the "merely offensive" words with which Charles Hardy discriminated against her could indeed constitute a violation of Title VII.[60]

With this precedent, it will surely be an uphill battle for those who advocate that free speech rights should prevail over equal protection rights. And that is as it should be. For in their desire to advance the First Amendment rights of those male workers who want to denigrate women, these advocates are willing to ignore or reduce the Fourteenth Amendment rights of those female workers who want the right to earn a livelihood unimpeded by discriminatory treatment, even discrimination created by "merely offensive" words. The Constitution's grand guarantee of "equal protection of the law" surely means that Congress can act to preserve the right of women to work free from discrimination so degrading that it can force many women to walk off the job rather than tolerate the intended humiliation. This is all the more so when we consider that the men who wish to denigrate women with sexually explicit language have not lost the right to do so. In the privacy of their homes, in public demonstrations and fora, in literature and movies, they may and do exercise that right. But they should not be able to hound a woman off the job or force her to endure humiliation in silence as a price for keeping her job. The law prohibiting sexual harassment is not a prudish attempt to silence the "merely offensive." Rather, it is a guarantee that women, like men, may earn their livelihood without discrimination and take their place in the public sphere of employment without fear or degradation.

■ Deborah Ellis

The conflict between speech and equality in the workplace has become a hot issue, at least in part because sexual harassment law is now addressing what I call the "second generation" employment discrimination cases. First generation cases focused on ending the *exclusion* of women from the workplace so that women could be hired or obtain promotions. Second generation cases address *conditions* in the workplace, thereby attempting to transform some of the male-centered norms that led to the exclusion. The goal is to create conditions in which true equality is possible, or in Title VII language, to change the "terms or conditions" of employment.

In trying to accommodate values of speech and equality, we should focus not only on the different kinds of speech, but on the different forums where speech occurs—in this case, the workplace.

At the outset, more than Professor Ross, I give greater credence to the legitimate desires of workers to express themselves in the workplace. Though Ross is generally correct that as a matter of current law, employers' rather than employees' speech rights are at issue in harassment cases, at least one civil liberties group, the ACLU, works to expand workers' rights in *many* different contexts: from eliminating drug testing to penalties for conduct outside the workplace, such as smoking. Thus it is worthwhile to consider initially whether the principles of the First Amendment argue for the expansion of workers' speech rights, including the right to engage in offensive speech.

Those who argue that harassing speech in the workplace should not be enjoined point out that part of the price of living in a free society is to tolerate speech that is highly offensive. Analogizing to the march of the Nazis through the Jewish suburb of Skokie,[61] they acknowledge that most people would not condone such speech, but point out that it is precisely speech "at the fringe" that needs protection. This is undoubtedly true. The First Amendment is not necessary to protect speech that the majority agrees with. Rather, like other provisions in the Bill of Rights, the First Amendment exists to protect minorities, which in this context are unpopular ideas.

Advocates for the primacy of free expression in the workplace go on to argue that women employees must accept the workplace as they find it and not be "politically correct" thought-police who tell other workers that their modes of expression are offensive. Because under this analysis one solution for offensive speech is "more speech," women employees should instead respond by expressing their own ideas. For example, if confronted with demeaning photos of nude women, women could post demeaning photos of nude men (if one could find such photos).

An example of this view is a 1991 law review article entitled "Title VII As Censorship" by Kingsley Browne.[62] In that article, Browne advocates that workplace speech expressing views about the qualities of certain groups, such as minorities or women, should be considered political speech in the same way that speech advocating nondiscriminatory treatment should be. Browne notes that courts have found that the more political the message, the more offensive it is. For example, the statement that "women belong in the bedroom and not the factory," is not only offensive but communicates a definite political viewpoint. Interestingly, Browne modifies his views somewhat for racial harassment cases, noting that the message in racial harassment cases is less ambiguous than that involved in the sexual context. The objectionable message in racial harassment cases is generally one of hostility and prejudice—racial slurs and epithets are common features—while in the sexual context, the message may be either hostile or sexual.

This distinction is illusory. The purported distinction illustrates Ross's point that the term sexual harassment has disserved women by putting too much focus on sexuality. The real message in sexual harassment, like racial harassment cases, is one of exclusion. A case the National Organization for Women Legal Defense and Education Fund (NOW LDEF) brought in Florida, *Robinson v. Jacksonville Shipyards*,[63] illustrates this point well.

In *Robinson*, NOW LDEF represented a woman welder, Lois Robinson, in a Title VII suit challenging the pornography and lewd comments she faced at a shipyard. Robinson is a first-class welder, one of the few women welders at the shipyard, and indeed one of the only female skilled craftsworkers in a workplace where "women craftsworkers are an extreme rarity."[64] For example, in 1980, the shipyard employed two women and 958 men as skilled craftsworkers; in

1986, the percentages had improved to six women out of 846 men.⁶⁵ The shipyard has never had a female supervisor.

After a trial, the district court cited many instances to support its findings of a hostile work environment. For example, Lois Robinson could not avoid the pervasive pornographic pictures in her workplace. They were posted where she worked, in the trailer where she picked up her tools; pictures were waved in her face and left on her toolbox. The pictures were explicit. They included photos of nude and seminude women in sexually suggestive or demeaning poses. One display was a dartboard with a woman's nipple as the bull's-eye; another was a woman's pubic area with a meat spatula pressed on it.

Some pictures were specifically targeted at Lois Robinson. For example, one picture that was waved in her face by a co-worker in an enclosed area where she worked was of a nude woman with long blonde hair wearing high heels and holding a whip. Robinson has long blonde hair and uses a welder's tool known as a whip. Not surprisingly, she felt particularly targeted by that picture.⁶⁶

Other women at the shipyards also experienced harassment by pornography. For example, two women were shown a picture of the infamous Long Dong Silver. In addition to the pictures, Lois Robinson also was subject to verbal harassment, such as a co-worker who said, "Hey pussycat, come here and give me a whiff." When Lois Robinson complained about these incidents, the complaint process became yet another occasion for harassment. Management told her that the shipyard is a "man's world" and agreed to remove only pictures of people having sex. In contrast, the foreman in charge of personnel testified at trial that he would probably throw any calendar with a picture of a nude man on it in the trash. Most telling, after a pornographic calendar on the shipyard trailer was removed in response to Robinson's complaints, a "men only" sign appeared on the trailer door. That sign declared explicitly what the pictures said implicitly.

This incident illustrates Ross's point that the term sexual harassment is a misnomer because sexual harassment in the workplace has little to do with sexuality and much to do with power. Women may no longer be explicitly barred from being welders, but harassment such as the pornography in *Robinson* communicates to women that they are not welcome in the male workplace.

Why shouldn't workers be able to communicate such a message of exclusion? As Browne points out, such a message is political, and political expression has long been protected by First Amendment principles. For me, the key reason is the nature of the workplace. In addition to the reasons set forth by Ross, regulated speech in the workplace is permissible precisely because a workplace is a place for work, not a forum for the exchange of ideas. Employees of private employers already have the limited speech the employer chooses to bestow. Public employees have more rights, but even for them courts have recognized that concern for speech must be balanced against the employers' interest in ensuring the effective functioning of the office.[67]

A central tenet of American free speech jurisprudence is the concept that the antidote to any speech with which one disagrees is counterspeech. As Justice Brandeis wrote in *Whitney v. California*,[68] the remedy for disagreeable speech "is more speech, not enforced silence." But in most workplaces, there is no realistic opportunity to counter with more speech because of the lack of significant numbers of women and the economic coercion of needing to earn a living.

Robinson illustrates why Brandeis's "more speech" antidote is unrealistic for most workers. At the shipyard, management had denied employees' requests to post political materials, advertisements, and commercial materials. It barred newspapers or other reading material due to safety concerns. Only one type of speech was allowed without prior approval: pictures of nude or seminude women.[69]

I think it is useful to picture forums on a spectrum, with parks and other traditional public forums at one end and the workplace at the other. In between are forums that are more difficult to categorize. For example, a university traditionally has been a place of robust debate, yet it is also necessary for the university to afford equal educational opportunity. Another point on the spectrum is a shopping mall, a forum that should be categorized as public for speech purposes. In our mobile, consumer-oriented society, the shopping mall in many communities has become the true town square, and yet the U.S. Supreme Court has refused to recognize a right of free speech there.[70]

Having said that the workplace is a forum where speech that excludes women should not be allowed, what should be the extent of permissible relief in a sexual harassment case? To remedy the discrimination at the shipyard, the trial judge in *Robinson* ordered a comprehensive remedy, including training of the shipyard workers, instituting policies and procedures to curb harassment, and a ban on posting pornography or bringing pornographic materials into the workplace. The ACLU filed an amicus brief in *Robinson* objecting to portions of this remedial relief on the grounds that it is overbroad, applies to material that is merely sexually suggestive, and bans nontargeted expressive activity. However, the NOW LDEF argues that the relief ordered must be viewed in light of the history of pervasive, deeply rooted sexual harassment at the shipyard and the broad principles of remedial relief in Title VII cases articulated by the Supreme Court in *Albemarle Paper Company v. Moody*.[71] As the Supreme Court explained in *Albemarle*, courts have a "duty to render a decree which will so far as possible eliminate the discriminatory effects of the past, as well as bar like discrimination in the future."

Courts' broad remedial powers under Title VII justify some infringement on constitutional rights if the remedy is narrowly tailored to serve a compelling government purpose. For example, courts have ordered remedial relief in hiring and promotion cases, such as a one-for-one promotion order, even when the Fourteenth Amendment equal protection rights of other employees are adversely effected.[72] Moreover, the remedial relief ordered in *Robinson* must be considered in light of the shipyard's history of banning all public displays of expressive activity except sexual materials. There are no alternative remedies because by the management's own admission, the shipyard is large and hard to monitor.

As someone committed to feminism and civil liberties, I value both speech and equality. But to argue that offensive speech should not be subject to Title VII's prohibition of a hostile environment does not take sufficient account of the realities for women employees. Those who want to express a sincere view that women do not belong in the workplace can engage in other modes of communication, from talking to neighbors to writing letters to the editor to lobbying legislators. Some would say that those options are not sufficient, for much of social interaction in the modern era occurs at work, not in the mythical town square. But that fact must be balanced against the economic reality that women must work in order to provide for themselves and their families. In *Rabidue*, a Sixth Circuit case, the Court used the fact of pornography and other discrimination women face in society as a reason they should "tough it out" at work; the court said that Title VII was "not designed to bring about a magical transformation in the social mores of American workers."[73] However, I think the *Robinson* court had the better view when it reiterated that "the whole point of the sexual harassment claim is that behavior that may be permissible in some settings can be abusive in the workplace."[74]

■ Wendy Kaminer

I agree with much of what Susan has said and probably end up in a similar place, but I'm going to try to be as disagreeable as possible anyway and set out a more restrictive way of considering hostile environment claims.

First of all, I don't agree that the First Amendment claims in these cases are specious. The argument about the centrality of the workplace in people's lives that is used to defend sexual harassment claims is also a defense of free speech claims. For people who spend a majority of their waking hours on the job, the workplace is an important forum for opinions and ideas and all the prejudices they entail. People develop the same kinds of relationships with their corporate employers that they have with their government, which is why we advocate for a range of workplace rights, including rights of speech. So a ban on pornography in the workplace is not, as Susan suggests, comparable to a time, place, and manner restriction. A ban on "offensive" speech is hardly content-neutral, and, given the primacy of the workplace as a forum, a pornography ban is more like a ban on streetcorner preaching than a rule prohibiting bullhorns in parades.

Free speech rights are also at risk in harassment cases because the harassment debate has become part of a larger debate about censorship of pornography. The arguments about the harm of pornography in the workplace, which are often raised in harassment debates, derive from arguments about the harm of pornography in general and the presumption that all women are invariably demeaned and subordinated by sexually explicit material marketed to men.

I don't want to fall into the trap that Susan has described of paying more attention to the sex part of these cases than the harassment part, and perhaps we should adopt some clunkier, less catchy term like "verbal gender discrimination." But in fact, sexual harassment cases, dating back over a hundred years, do involve sex as well as gender. They're cases about women being propositioned or sexually intimidated by their supervisors, or they're cases about pornography. Today, feminist defenses of hostile environment cases, in which the harassment is not clearly targeted, are often arguments against pornography. They boil down to the notion that pornography is inherently discriminatory. Putting a picture of a nude woman in an erotic pose on a company bulletin board is compared to putting up a picture of a lynching.

So you walk a very fine line, politically, when you oppose efforts of some feminists to censor pornography while you support efforts to prohibit untargeted, verbal harassment. It's impossible to take the First Amendment out of this debate, although it may not always trump women's rights.

That being said, however, I do agree that we need to recognize hostile environment claims based on untargeted speech, because if we only recognize clearly targeted verbal harassment, we're only recognizing clearly intentional harassment. Not targeting your sexism, making cracks about women in general, instead of one woman in particular, is a good way of cloaking your discriminatory intent. The hostile environment rule has been compared to the disparate impact rule in Title VII cases, because it allows us to reach behavior with discriminatory effects when discriminatory intent is impossible to prove.

There are, then, dangers in the notion, endorsed by Feminists for Free Expression, that we should limit liability to intentional discrimination in cases involving speech. It would not only provide a subterfuge for sexual harassment but could also legitimize limitations on claims of effective discrimination in general. Dispensing with a hostile environment standard might be like dispensing with a prohibition of standardized tests that serve to exclude women or minority males from higher paying jobs.

So it's a challenge trying to figure out a hostile environment rule that doesn't rely on some vague notion of offensive speech and doesn't endorse feminist critiques of pornography. What drives a lot of people crazy about feminist discussions of harassment, myself included, is the popular notion that a woman who feels offended has been harassed. One student suggested to me last year that harassment is making someone feel uncomfortable; she then prescribed a set of remedies for generating discomfort, ranging from compulsory re-education to suspension to firing. I hate to think where that would leave me, because I make people feel uncomfortable almost every day. I feel as if I've failed if I haven't made someone uncomfortable in the course of a day. Sexual harassment has to mean something more than making people uncomfortable or offending them. But what you hear in some feminist discussions of harassment is the notion that the idiosyncratic sensibilities of a particular woman plaintiff should be the primary measure of discrimination. Implicit in the proposal that we should replace a reasonable person with a reasonable woman standard is the notion that we should dispense with the standard of reasonableness entirely and rely on the subjective reaction of the woman plaintiff. Her feelings become the facts of the case.

Feelings are facts in a therapist's office, but not in a court of law. What's troubling about the harassment debate in general is its tendency to confuse law and therapy, the dangers of which were made clear by the rule at issue in the *Harris* case requiring women to show serious psychological harm to sustain a harassment claim. That's too high a standard for women who are emotionally resilient, and too low a standard for women who are easily traumatized. It's much too subjective a standard and plays into the increasingly popular notion that women are emotionally weak, easily disabled by sexist remarks and by pornography.

In cases involving speech, it's crucial to objectify the hostile environment standard as much as possible, however unfashionable the notion of objectivity might be. Obviously the use of a reasonable person standard, which I prefer to a reasonable woman standard, is one way to protect against wholesale prohibition of offensive speech. It's not an impossible standard to apply. If we can objectify claims of self-defense, involving subjective apprehensions of harm, with a reasonable person standard, we can objectify claims of verbal harassment. In addition, we can require evidence of objective harm—effect on job performance or advancement—as we require evidence of objective harm in libel cases. Finally, we can require an examination of the objective context of the harassment claim.

There are, I think, at least three factors to consider: (1) the history of women in the occupation or trade at issue; (2) the number of women in the workplace at issue; and (3) the distribution of men and women in the workplace hierarchy. What I'm suggesting is that a hostile environment claim raised by a woman in a workplace dominated or occupied more or less equally by women should have little credibility, on its face, unless women are relegated to lower-level jobs and men have a lock on management. It seems obvious that the cases with which we ought to be most concerned are those involving workplaces in which women still constitute a minority with relatively little power. And of course those are the workplaces in which the most grievous cases of untargeted harassment will occur. Those are the cases in which the right not to be harassed may outweigh the right to air your prejudices.

■ Discussion

SUSAN DELLER ROSS: I'd like to make clear that I am not someone who believes in banning or censoring pornography. In fact, I have signed a brief saying we should not do so.[75] But I do think it's possible—and many of us do—to take the position that one is both anticensorship in terms of the whole antipornography movement and antidiscrimination in the workplace, because that's a very different context.

Wendy Kaminer talked about a student who thought sexual harassment was what was sexually offensive to her; that example shows that one of the problems with sexual harassment as a label is that people think they know what it means, but they don't. You don't see the kind of argument the student was making in the federal courts. There, lawyers have to prove there was discrimination based on gender in working conditions. Those are the statutory terms: working conditions, and differences based on gender. So for those cases, you have to show that women are being treated differently than men—without that, you don't have a sex discrimination case.

So if you have, hypothetically, pictures in one workplace of nude men who are sexually aroused and in erotic positions, and pictures of nude women in equally sexually aroused and erotic positions, you don't have a case, in my view, under Title VII. But the reality is there aren't any such workplaces.

I suppose one form of cure for this particular problem is to say we're going to ensure that there are really erotic poses of men up there on the workplace walls. We'll go around to all the walls and for every nude female, we'll put up a nude male. If the employers want to do that, they can do it. I guarantee you that there won't be many employers who'll take us up on it.

Finally, these cases are not about mere offensiveness. To win a sexual harassment case under Title VII you have to show first that the offensive language is only directed at one sex and not at the other; second, that it's sexual in nature; third, that it's unwelcome, and that the woman has indicated that it's unwelcome; and fourth, that it is severe or pervasive.

I believe that is all the objective test that we need. We don't need this "reasonableness" screen, which is nothing more than a subjective concept. It's couched as an objective term, but in fact all it is is a label for some white male judges' gut intuitive judgement about what people should have to tolerate. Those judges have not had to endure the kinds of name-calling that Vivienne Rabidue had to endure. That's a reality that most men just haven't experienced in their lives. They have never had to encounter being called these kinds of demeaning terms over and over and over on a daily basis at work. It's simply not part of their experience.

WENDY KAMINER: I'm trying to describe a political problem, not a legal problem. The political problem is that the way the courts define sexual harassment is not going to be clearly understood or clearly talked about. You get this general sense, and I hear it from a lot of feminists and a lot of students, that sexual harassment is *Playboy* calendars in the workplace. And that the mere display of pin-ups is or should be enough for a sexual harassment case. Some women, especially if they have some sort of abuse in their background, may claim that they suffer from posttraumatic stress disorder and are deeply wounded by sexually explicit materials in the workplace. We have to find a way to support sexual harassment claims without encouraging women to feel traumatized by pornography. It's not enough to say, "That's not exactly what the federal courts are doing." That might solve the legal problem, but it doesn't address the larger political question.

ROSS: You're quite right that there's an education problem. Employers and institutions need to hire very good lawyers to run very good training sessions on just what is prohibited and what is not. That's what employers ordinarily do when the Supreme Court or the Congress announces a new law that binds the employers: They learn what the standard really requires. They work very carefully within the confines of the law and it's within employers' capabilities to do just that.

KAMINER: But there's also a certain amount of overreaction going on in places of employment. I think it's fair to talk about the chilling effect of sexual harassment law as a problem that we have to address. In everything that you've said, Susan, I can still see a lot of cases in which harassment will come down to prohibiting pornography in the workplace, and I have a problem with that.

DEBORAH ELLIS: I would take a different tack on this. It's easy to say, "Oh, there are a lot of employers who are banning pornography in the workplace," but I don't think that's probably happening. I don't think a lot of people are filing spurious sex discrimination claims. People are always very concerned about the hypersensitive plaintiffs, but I'm not so sure there are many cases of the hypersensitive plaintiff, which is why Susan is right to focus on what's really happening in the federal courts. How many hypersensitive women are there out there? Lois Robinson's case is the only case in the country concerning pornography in the workplace, and in that case the court concluded that the hostile environment that had been proved was very much connected to other conditions in the workplace such as the rarity of women and the hierarchical relationships in the workplace.

NADINE STROSSEN: The *Robinson* case is the only case in which we have a judicial opinion on the particular legal issue. Anecdotally, I can report from my travels around college campuses misunderstandings and misguided enforcement of the concept of sexual harassment that doesn't even get to the level of filing a complaint in a federal court, let alone an administrative proceeding or a judicial opinion. The culture is reflecting a much looser standard of sexual harassment.

ELLIS: That's on campuses, not the workplace.

STROSSEN: I've heard anecdotes from workplaces as well. My own experience happens to be more on campuses. But we should not mistake what popular understanding is, especially because we don't have countervailing First Amendment protections with respect to most workplaces and with respect to some campuses. There's going to be an underprotection of free speech because there is no legal backstop there.

I don't know how useful it is to give examples, but one that many people have heard about was from Pennsylvania State University last year. A female faculty member was teaching a course in a classroom that happened to be mostly used for art courses, and therefore there were reproductions of famous paintings of nude women. She complained that that created a hostile and intimidating environment for her on the basis of gender. I don't think she even instituted a formal complaint, but the university capitulated and removed the paintings from the wall. And there are many similar such incidents.

KAMINER: Part of our problem in having this discussion is that we don't have a lot of good empirical information about what the cases look like that don't make it to federal court. What kind of complaints are state antidiscrimination offices hearing? What kind of complaints are supervisors hearing in their offices, taking steps to address before anyone files a formal complaint anywhere or before anyone ever hears about the case?

STEVE POLAN: I've been involved in trying to grapple with some of these issues as a manager in both the public sector and the private sector. Frequently, a situation arises in which there is a perceived problem of harassment which doesn't rise to the legal standard of harassment. Yet, how do you balance that problem when you want to discipline the employees who are involved and they raise a First Amendment objection. "I can do this," they say, "this is not harassment as defined by the courts." Yet it's highly objectionable behavior to public sector management. That's where the issue gets very tough in terms of the First Amendment. None of you have commented on that because you all presume that the legal definition of harassment has been satisfied.

ROSS: I don't think Title VII helps you there. If it doesn't violate Title VII, I don't see how you can use Title VII as a justification for disciplining the employees. You have to come up instead with management criteria that deal with the actual behavior that you—as managers—feel justified in prohibiting, whether or not Title VII requires you to prohibit it, and that you can support on First Amendment grounds if you are operating in the public sector. But if it's not sex-based, it's not illegal under Title VII.

ELLIS: Of course public employers are a little less free to fire people for any reason they want to. The majority of employment in this country is at-will employment, and employers have always felt free to regulate speech in the workplace.

ROSS: Deborah's right. Not only do employers regulate speech without violating the First Amendment, the government also regulates employers' speech without violating the First Amendment. In fact, there's a 1969 Supreme Court case, *NLRB v. Gissel Packing Co.*,[76] which involves an employer threatening people who are trying to organize a union, threatening that if they go ahead and organize a union, it's going to be very tough for them. The NLRB tells him he may not speak in that way. He defends himself on First Amendment grounds, and the case goes up to the Supreme Court, which holds that even the *employer's* speech is not protected speech under the First Amendment.

Let me go on to a different point. I think these people with strong First Amendment concerns are misled about the nature of sexual harassment cases. People really get misled by the label of sexuality. They believe the cases are about sex and that women workers are just trying to suppress "dirty" sexual speech. I originally thought that sexual harassment was not a very significant issue, until I began reading the cases the women brought. The cases are not part of a political campaign to get clean language in the workplace. It's clear that frequently, the words some of these men use represent nothing less than a concerted campaign to get women out of the workplace. The disgusting level of behavior is just incredible, and it's done with words. It's done by writing "cavern cunt" in the dust of a car window because the car belongs to one of three women who've just been hired to be a flag person on a previously all-male highway construction crew.[77] The intent behind those words is to drive the women off, and it does drive them off. We shouldn't kid ourselves that just because it's about words, it's not about jobs. Lots of women are going to hear about that particular road construction crew and they're going to say, "I don't want to go work there. It ain't worth it, even though I could make a lot more money there than I could typing." The reason we have all these constructive discharge cases is that the women can't take it. They leave the job, saying, "It's not worth it to me to live the way I'm living." Teresa Harris said, "I cried at night. I drank too much to get myself to sleep so I could go to work the next day." Her job performance wasn't affected. They thought she was a terrific manager. She got promotions and bonuses. But she couldn't take it. Words have a real impact on people.

And these words affect many women. Lots of Charles Hardy's speech was directed to all his women employees. The trial judge ruled that he was demeaning to women in general, but that some of the clerical workers were conditioned to accept it. That kind of effect presents a danger in terms of the reasonable woman standard: Employers are going to get up in court, if we have a reasonable woman standard, and say, "Fifty-six percent of the women in this workplace don't find this insulting, so it's okay." The fact that some women tolerate it will be used to suggest that the women who oppose it are hypersensitive and unreasonable.

DAVID COLE: We often confuse, in talking about sexism and gender discrimination, sex and gender. It seems to me that the analogy to a racially hostile work environment is a gender-based hostile work environment, not a hostile work environment of a sexual nature.

And so the question is, Why is the legal requirement "of a sexual nature"? Wouldn't it be better if we called it gender harassment rather than sexual harassment? It seems to me that there are two reasons that "of a sexual nature" is in there, or might be in there. One is that legally it makes it easier to justify regulating speech because the Supreme Court has often treated sexual speech much less sympathetically under the First Amendment than political speech, and so we characterize it as sexual, which is easier to regulate.

From a political standpoint, focusing on the sexual nature also makes it easier for the same reason that Catherine MacKinnon can get right-wing support for her views—because we have a history of wanting to suppress sexuality in our society. That history has played an important role in the subordination of women. There's a notion that linking women and sex is improper, or that women being explicit about sex is improper. To the extent that we call it sexual harassment, we support a definition that requires that it be of a sexual nature, and we are playing into the kind of concerns that Wendy Kaminer is talking about. Why can't it just be called gender harassment, and take out the sexuality?

ROSS: It could be, and I agree with your basic point. Interestingly, when Justice Ruth Bader Ginsburg was questioning the lawyers in *Harris* she asked, "If a women has to put up with something on her job that a man doesn't have to, isn't that just a difference based on gender in her working conditions?" I would say that sexual harassment is just a subset of cases involving a difference in working conditions based on gender.

The reason there's a separate set of guidelines about it, and that those guidelines require a sexual content, is that it's important where sex is concerned to differentiate welcome behavior from unwelcome. Obviously, there are many people who are sexually attracted to one another in workplaces, and Title VII doesn't attempt to ban that. So the sexual harassment guidelines apply only when sexual overtures or remarks are made to or denigrate persons of one sex, the overtures or remarks are unwelcome, they're turned down, they're persistent, and the recipient of the unwanted sexuality gets hurt as a result, whether by being forced off the job or intimidated into enduring humiliating treatment in silence.

The courts have had no difficulty in treating some of the comments that Charles Hardy made to Teresa Harris as simply gender-based comments, such as "You're a dumb woman, what do you know?" That remark has no sexual content, so it wouldn't fall into the sexual harassment guidelines. But on the other hand, it would be viewed as a simple case of discrimination in working conditions because of gender under Title VII, and that's the way the courts have treated it.

KAMINER: You can't take the sex out of sexual harassment, though, because so many of these cases are about sex, not about gender. We've been saying that if we had a workplace in which there were pictures of nude men as well as nude women you wouldn't have a harassment case, but there are an awful lot of feminists who would disagree with that because they would say that women are intimidated by nude photographs in a way that men are not because of the ways in which women are objectified and because of the epidemic of sexual violence. For many women, sexual harassment is about sex.

ROSS: Well, I'd probably write a brief opposing them.

ELLIS: I would strongly disagree too. I don't think that the pornographic pictures are about sex, they're about excluding women and about power. It has nothing to do with sex.

KAMINER: That really is just semantics. Pornography is sexually explicit material. It has everything to do with sex. That's why is arouses so much opposition. And the primary feminist argument against pornography is that it encourages sexual violence and the sexual abuse of women.

SYLVIA LAW: Because I think we know something about the prevalence of sexual harassment, and I think that the example Nadine Strossen offered is both trivializing and extremely class-based, I want to add something. I spent many years working with a group called Non-Traditional Employment for Women, and at least in blue-collar service work, in less elite work, it is just a pervasive problem. We know, for example, that more than 90 percent of the claims that come to the New York State Attorney General's Office are claims of gender harassment, often of a sexual form, mostly in blue-collar work.

ELLIS: It's not a coincidence that these claims come in places where women are excluded from the workplace. Another example of that, in addition to *Robinson*, is a case that was litigated by the Women's Rights Clinic at New York University Law School, the Brenda Berkman case, where Professor Laura Sager and students worked to have women admitted as firefighters in New York City. Once they succeeded, they had to bring a sexual harassment case because the women were harassed. They weren't harassed with pornography there; they were harassed, as I remember, with feces and bras stuffed in their boots. It was a not-too-subtle way of barring women from the workplace once they got over the hurdle of the physical exams.

ROSS: But remember that if an employer maintains dirty, disgusting toilets for both men and women, it's not illegal. Title VII is not a general directive to clean up the workplace, to make it real nice for everybody. It's about discrimination.

JULIE NOVKOV: Part of what is going on here is a disagreement about what constitutes an injury and how we go about showing that an injury has in fact occurred. If we can think about the reasonable woman standard as providing a way of bringing women's perspectives into the definition of an injury, it can actually provide more of a prophylactic than Ms. Ross has suggested.

I agree that we have to be careful that it doesn't get co-opted and create a higher standard that women have to reach in order to show that sexual harassment has occurred. What constitutes injury in fact? Do you have to show that there has been some detriment in work performance or psychological injury, as opposed to just showing that the intent behind the discrimination has been to drive women out of the workplace in a particular setting?

KAMINER: If you had a clear showing of intent the case would be easy. You're right that the problem is trying to define the injury and to set standards for the injury. That's what drives everybody nuts. I'm not personally in favor of a reasonable woman standard as opposed to a reasonable person standard partly because I associate it with a history of protective laws for women.

The other thing that makes me uncomfortable about the reasonable woman standard is that while we haven't talked about other kinds of harassment, I'm assuming that a lot of the principles that we're talking about here would apply to racial harassment or harassment based on religion or sexual orientation. I would hate to see us get to the point where we talk about reasonable women, and reasonable African Americans, and reasonable gay people, and we end up in a way saying that the only people who are plain old reasonable people are white males, so that a standard that's supposed to be undermining the male norm begins to provide another kind of foundation for it.

ROSS: Actually, there's an interesting disparity in the law, which is that reasonableness has not been used in the area of race discrimination. It's an actual injury test—that is, if the *actual* victim was offended, that's all she or he needs to win the case. If you're called "nigger, nigger, nigger" five times a day, the courts don't say, "Would a reasonable black person find this offensive?" Nor do they require that the black employee be either psychologically injured or that his or her job performance be affected in order to win a court case. An employee in that position can be a very strong person. She can grit her teeth and do a superb job, but does she have to be treated that way when white employees aren't called similar epithets? The courts say, "No, that's race discrimination in her working conditions."

MARTIN REDISH: We've been talking primarily about gender-based discrimination, but obviously Title VII isn't limited that way. So what do you do with the indirect hostile environment in other contexts? For example, what if an employee puts a picture of George Wallace over his desk and another African-American employee is intimidated by that? Would that be considered racial harassment, and if so, where does the First Amendment come into play?

ROSS: I can't think of any such cases ever being brought. If you look at the cases that have been brought, they involve nasty racial epithets, or the noose hanging over a black employee's desk—that's the kind of case that gets brought.

REDISH: But I'm asking what the difference is between a nondirected or nontargeted pin-up and a nontargeted or

148   Discussion

nondirected picture of George Wallace. Isn't each equally intimidating to the particular group protected by Title VII?

ELLIS: Wait a minute, George Wallace has reformed you know.

REDISH: David Duke, then. I'm sorry, I'm behind the times. You miss the paper one day and George Wallace has reformed.

ROSS: I think a better hypothetical would be a picture of a black man hanging from a tree with a noose around his neck that the white employee hangs on his wall, and all the black employees have to see it every time they walk by.

REDISH: That might be an interesting example, but it's not the point I'm trying to make. I was trying to raise questions about the intersection between an individual's right to express political viewpoints, as offensive as they may be, and the interest of an individual of a statutorily protected minority group who might be intimidated as a result of it. I'm wondering whether in the pin-up case we're not ignoring the First Amendment, whereas in the George Wallace or the David Duke case, we would say the First Amendment comes into play despite its intimidating effect. I'm wondering whether we're not pushing the First Amendment under the rug when it comes to the nondirected pin-up case, when in many ways, it's not that different from the nondirected picture of David Duke.

ROSS: Well, what about my hypothetical? The picture of the black man hanging from a tree being lynched and it's not directed at any individual, it's just hanging on your wall as an expression of your genuine beliefs about blacks.

REDISH: Tough case. I probably would, if that's all we're talking about.

ROSS: That's all we're talking about, but every single day you have to see it, and it's your boss who's put it up.

REDISH: I would probably say that it's protected. It's unlikely it would be all that's going on. Somebody who's going to put that up is going to be doing a lot more than that. If it's part and parcel of a targeted, visual, coercive harassment scheme, then I would think it's not protected.

QUESTION: One of the problems with the discussion is that there is an over-assumption of the availability of freedom of speech in the workplace. It's not too often that a worker would address his supervisor as "boy" and not be disciplined for it. It's not often that a worker will habitually use crude language in addressing the CEO of the company and not be disciplined for it.

The workplace for many people is a place of temporary abode. Depending on the environment, you can get away from it during your breaks, get away from it during meal periods. You're not there prior to the worktime; you're not there after the worktime. Perhaps this makes the problem more complex, but it seems to me that the focal policy choice of Title VII is an economic one. We want full access to the workplace for all people, based on their ability to perform whatever work is available and not on the basis of particular kinds of prejudgments that either those who do the work or do the recruiting have, or that fellow employees have.

Now, since work so often carries with it all sorts of restrictions on expression, perhaps the reasonable person test is an appropriate way of enforcing the economic right of access to the work market, since this is already an area of restricted speech in the first place.

ROSS: What we hear in this dialogue is a desire for more free speech rights in general for workers, but they don't now exist. In truth, private employees don't have free speech rights on the job, so an essential policy value being suggested here by some people is to get more free speech rights for workers while they're on the job. But why do we start with this particular issue—with expanding free speech rights on the job for men who want to sexually denigrate women workers? That seems like a very peculiar place to start a campaign for more free speech rights for workers.

Notes

1. See, e.g., *New York Times v. Sullivan,* 376 U.S. 254 (1964), *NAACP v. Claiborne Hardware* 459 U.S. 898 (1982), *NAACP v. Button,* 371 U.S. 415 (1963), *NAACP v. Alabama,* 357 U.S. 449 (1958), *Dombrowski v. Pfister,* 380 U.S. 479 (1965), *Brown v. Louisiana,* 383 U.S. 131 (1966), and *Gregory v. City of Chicago,* 394 U.S. 111 (1969).

2. See, e.g., *Grayned v. Rockford,* 408 U.S. 104 (1972).

3. *Chaplinsky v. New Hampshire,* 315 U.S. 568 (1942), is the classic case, holding that words designed and intended to cause immediate violence are not protected by the First Amendment. Despite substantial criticism, it has never been rejected by the Court. See, e.g., *R.A.V. v. City of St. Paul,* 112 S. Ct. 2538 (1992).

4. See Stanley K. Henshaw, "Factors Hindering Access to Abortion Services," 27 Fam. Plan. Persp. 54 (1995). See also *Pro-Choice Network v. Project Rescue,* 799 F. Supp. 1417 (W.D.N.Y. 1992) (providing a vivid summary of incidents of clinic violence).

5. 437 U.S. 483 (1978). Union organizers may solicit members in a hospital workers' cafeteria but not in patient care areas because "the primary function of a hospital is patient care," and "a tranquil atmosphere is essential to the carrying out of that function." (Brennan for a unanimous Court.)

6. Contrast *Amalgamated Food Employees Local 590 v. Logan Valley Plaza,* 391 U.S. 308 (1968) (protecting union members' right to picket in a shopping mall), with *Lloyd Corp v. Tanner,* 407 U.S. 551 (1972) (denying war protesters the right to leaflet in a mall).

7. *Cox v. Louisiana,* 379 U.S. 559 (1965).

8. *Grayned v. Rockford,* 408 U.S. 104 (1972).

9. FACE provides civil remedies and criminal penalties against

"who[m]ever—by force or threat of force or by physical obstruction, intentionally injures, intimidates or interferes with" any person who is or has been "obtaining or providing reproductive health services." 18 U.S.C. Sec. 248 (1994). Abortion opponents have challenged the federal law as beyond congressional authority under the Commerce Clause and as unconstitutional under the First Amendment. Courts have rejected these challenges. See, e.g., *American Life League v. Reno*, 855 F. Supp. 137 (E.D. Va/. 1994); *United States v. Brock*, 863 F. Supp. 851 (E.D. Wis. 1994).

10. *Madsen v. Women's Health Center, Inc.*, 114 S. Ct. 2516 (1994).

11. *Id.* at 2528.

12. *Id.* at 2529.

13. In upholding the buffer zone, the Court noted the distinction between focused picketing and other types of generally disseminated communication, such as handbilling and solicitation, that cannot be banned in public places. In this case, the picketing was directed primarily at staff and patients, not the general public.

14. The Court found that injunctions "carry greater risks of censorship and discriminatory application."

15. The Court did strike down portions of the buffer zone that applied to areas where the clinic property was adjacent to private property. The Court found that there was no evidence that the buffer zone was needed in these areas, and thus the restriction was too broad.

16. The question of whether restrictions on antichoice protesters are content-based has been settled by the Supreme Court in *Madsen v. Women's Health Center*. The Court held that such restrictions in the context of injunctions are content neutral.

17. Since this paper was delivered, Congress has enacted the Freedom of Access to Clinic Entrances Acts, which imposes both criminal and civil penalties on anyone attempting through force, threat of force, or physical obstruction to impede access to reproductive health care.

18. Some state supreme courts, such as the Supreme Court of Massachusetts in the case of *Planned Parenthood League of Massachusetts, Inc., et al. v. Operation Rescue, et al.*, have rejected the

analysis in *Bray v. Alexandria Women's Health Clinic* and found that their state civil rights laws, although similar to the federal statute at issue in *Bray*, did protect women and clinics.

19. Indeed, the lack of response to antichoice campaigns of force and violence have led to escalating violence culminating in the recent murders in Massachusetts and Florida.

20. 42 U.S.C. §§ 2000e-2017 (1988).

21. U.S. Equal Employment Opportunity Commission, Guidelines on Discrimination Because of Sex, 29 C.F.R. § 1604.11(a)(1992).

22. *Barnes v. Train*, 13 Fair Empl. Prac. Cas. (BNA) 123, 124 (D.D.C. 1974), *rev'd sub nom.; Barnes v. Costle*, 561 F.2d 983 (D.C. Cir. 1977).

23. *Barnes v. Costle*, 561 F.2d 983 (D.C. Cir. 1977); *Tomkins v. Pub. Serv. Elec. & Gas Co.*, 568 F.2d 1044 (3rd Cir. 1977); *Garber v. Saxon Business Prods., Inc.*, 552 F.2d 1032 (4th Cir. 1977)(per curiam); *Corne v. Bausch & Lomb, Inc.*, 562 F.2d 55 (9th Cir. 1977), *vacating without op.*, 390 F. Supp. 161 (D. Ariz. 1975).

24. *Meritor Savings Bank v. Vinson*, 477 U.S. 57 (1986).

25. EEOC guidelines, 29 C.F.R. § 1604.11(a)(3)(1992)(emphasis added).

26. *Rabidue v. Osceola Refining Co.*, 805 F. 2d 611 (6th Cir. 1986), *cert. denied*, 481 U.S. 1041 (1987).

27. 805 F.2d at 620–21.

28. *Harris v. Forklift Systems, Inc.*, 60 Empl. Prac. Dec. (CCH) 42,070 at 74,250 (M.D. Tenn. 1990), *adopted*, 61 Fair Empl. Prac. Cas. (BNA) 240 (M.D. Tenn. 1991), *aff'd without op.*, 976 F.2d 733 (6th Cir. 1992), *rev'd*, 114 S.Ct. 367 (1993).

29. *Id.* at 74,249–50.

30. *Id.* at 74,250.

31. Brief for Petitioner at 4–5, *Harris v. Forklift Systems, Inc.*, 114 S.Ct. 367 (1993)(No. 92–1168)(citations omitted).

32. *Id.* at 8. *Webster's Third International Dictionary of the English Language Unabridged* 291 (1986) defines *buggery* as "unnatural sexual intercourse: SODOMY."

33. Brief Amicus Curiae of the American Civil Liberties Union

and the American Jewish Congress in Support of Petitioner at 6, *Harris* (No. 92–1168).

34. *Id.* at 6, 13–19; Brief of Amicus Curiae Feminists for Free Expression in Support of Petitioner at 6–7, 9, 17–18, 29–31, *Harris* (No. 92–1168).

35. Brief for Respondent at 33, *Harris* (No. 92–1168). See also *id.* at 7, 12–13 (favorably quoting ACLU/AJC and Feminists for Free Expression briefs proposing that plaintiffs be limited to cases of either job performance effect or psychological injury), 23–33. The ACLU/AJC and FFE briefs had been filed on April 30, 1993, as theoretically "in support of" Teresa Harris. The employer's brief citing them was filed June 1, 1993.

36. Brief Amici Curiae of the NAACP Legal Defense and Education Fund, Inc., and the National Council of Jewish Women in Support of Petitioner at 24, *Harris* (No. 92–1168).

37. Brief of the Women's Legal Defense Fund, the National Women's Law Center (additional Amici Curiae listed on inside cover) as Amici Curiae in Support of Petitioner at 24–25, n. 22 (citation omitted), *Harris* (No. 92–1168). (The author was of counsel on this brief.)

38. *Frisby v. Schultz*, 487 U.S. 474 (1988).

39. 487 U.S. at 487. See also *Madsen v. Women's Health Center, Inc.*, 114 S. Ct. 2516, 2528–30 (1994)(upholding a thirty-six-foot buffer zone and noise restrictions at an abortion clinic and noting that the "First Amendment does not demand that patients at a medical facility undertake Herculean efforts to escape the cacophony of political protests," but striking down a ban on "images observable" within clinic because "it is much easier for the clinic to pull its curtains than for the patient to stop up her ears"; also striking down a ban on picketing within three hundred feet of clinic staff members' residences, but suggesting that a narrower ban such as that in *Frisby* was permissible: "it appears that a limitation on the time, duration of picketing, and number of pickets outside a smaller zone could have accomplished the desired result"); *FCC v. Pacifica Foundation*, 438 U.S. 726, 748–49 (1978)(plurality opinion) ("To say that one may avoid further offense by turning off the radio

when he hears indecent language is like saying that the remedy for an assault is to run away after the first blow."); *Lehman v. City of Shaker Heights*, 418 U.S. 298, 306–7 (1974) (plurality opinion)("[I]f we are to turn a bus or a streetcar into either a newspaper or a park, we take great liberties with people who because of necessity become commuters and at the same time captive viewers or listeners.").

40. *Renton v. Playtime Theatres, Inc.*, 475 U.S. 41, 49 (1986)(quoting *Young v. American Mini Theatres, Inc.*, 427 U.S. 50, 71, n. 34 [1976][plurality opinion]).

41. *Id.* at 48 (quoting *Young*, 427 U.S. at 82, n.4)(Powell, J., concurring).

42. *May v. Evansville-Vanderburgh School Corp.*, 787 F.2d 1105, 1110, 1117 (7th Cir. 1986)(in setting where court found that school was not used for "meetings unrelated to school business.").

43. *NLRB v. Gissel Packing Co., Inc.*, 395 U.S. 575, 617 (1969).

44. *Ellis v. Brotherhood of Railway, Airline, & S.S. Clerks*, 466 U.S. 435, 455–56 (1984).

45. *Roberts v. United States Jaycees*, 468 U.S. 609, 623–24 (1984)("Minnesota's compelling interest in eradicating discrimination against its female citizens justifies the impact that application of the [Minnesota human rights] statute to the Jaycees may have on the male members' associational freedoms"; the State's "strong historical commitment to eliminating discrimination and assuring its citizens equal access to publicly available goods and services" represent "compelling state interests of the highest order.").

46. Section 1 of the Fourteenth Amendment prohibits states from denying equal protection of the laws to any person, while §5 gives Congress authority to "enforce, by appropriate legislation, the provisions of this [Amendment]." There is no doubt that Congress can act pursuant to §5 to ban discrimination by public employers, because it is the state itself that discriminates in that case. The Court's rulings on the scope of Congress's §5 authority, however, leave unsettled the extent to which that authority reaches the *private* sector. *Katzenbach v. Morgan*, 384 U.S. 641 (1966), *Heart of Atlanta Motel, Inc. v. United States*, 379 U.S. 241 (1964), and *Adarand Constructors, Inc. v. Pena*, 115 S. Ct. 2097 (1995) all could be read to

give support to the proposition, but do not hold, that Congress has §5 authority to reach private-sector employment discrimination as well as that in the public sector.

In *Heart of Atlanta Motel*, the Court both upheld the commerce clause-based constitutionality of Title II of the 1964 Civil Rights Act (which also contains Title VII) to reach discrimination in the private sector (in the operation of a motel of "purely local character") and reserved the possibility that Congress also had Fourteenth Amendment constitutional power to reach the private sector. Thus, the Court first acknowledged that "The legislative history of the Act indicates that Congress based the Act on §5 and the Equal Protection Clause of the Fourteenth Amendment as well as its power to regulate interstate commerce." *Heart of Atlanta Motel*, 379 U.S. at 249. The Court then upheld Congress's exercise of its commerce clause authority and went on to refuse to rule out the constitutionality of Congress's exercise of its §5 authority: "This is not to say that the remaining [§5] authority upon which it acted was not adequate, a question upon which we do not pass, but merely that since the commerce power is sufficient for our decision here we have considered it alone." *Id.* at 250.

An examination of the different opinions in *Adarand Constructors, Inc. v. Pena*, 115 S. Ct. 2097 (1995), also suggests that at least five members of the current Supreme Court (Justices Ginsburg, Stevens, Souter, Breyer, and O'Connor), and possibly more, could adhere to a broad reading of Congress's §5 authority to ban private-sector gender and race discrimination. See *id.* at 2134 and n. 1 (dissenting opinion of Justice Ginsburg, joined by Justice Breyer) (agreeing with Justice Stevens that "large deference is owed by the Judiciary to 'Congress's institutional competence and constitutional authority to overcome historic racial subjugation' " and favorably citing Justices Douglas and Goldberg's concurring *Heart of Atlanta Motel* opinions upholding Congress's exercise of its §5 authority). See also *Adarand*, 115 S. Ct. at 2126 and n. 11 (dissenting opinion of Justice Stevens, joined by Justice Ginsburg)("We have read §5 as a positive grant of authority to Congress, not just to punish violations, but also to define and expand the scope of the Equal Protection Clause.

Katzenbach v. Morgan, 384 U.S. 641 [1966]."); *Adarand*, 115 S. Ct. at 2132–33 (dissenting opinion of Justice Souter, joined by Justices Ginsburg and Breyer) (Congress may act under §5 to rectify private-sector discrimination that has been "subject to government acquiescence, with effects that remain" and quoting Justice O'Connor's concurring opinion in *Missouri v. Jenkins*, 115 S. Ct. 2038, 2061 [1995]["("Congress . . . enjoys ' "discretion in determining whether and what legislation is needed to secure the guarantees of the Fourteenth Amendment," ' (citation omitted) (quoting Katzenbach v. Morgan, 384 U.S., at 651)"]"). See also, *Adarand*, 115 S. Ct. at 2114, 2117 (Justice O'Connor's opinion for the Court)("It is true that various Members of this Court have taken different views of the authority §5 of the Fourteenth Amendment confers upon Congress to deal with the problem of racial discrimination, and the extent to which courts should defer to Congress' exercise of that authority.... We need not, and do not, address these differences today. For now, it is enough to observe that Justice Stevens' suggestion that any Member of this Court has repudiated in this case his or her previously expressed views on the subject . . . is incorrect."); ("The unhappy persistence of both the practice and the lingering effects of racial discrimination against minority groups in this country is an unfortunate reality, and government is not disqualified from acting in response to it.").

While Justice O'Connor obviously does not believe that §5 shields Congress from strict scrutiny of legislation giving explicit race or gender-based preferences, she also has supported relatively generous interpretation of Title VII insofar as it *eradicates* sex or race-based discrimination. See, e.g., *UAW v. Johnson Controls, Inc.*, 449 U.S. 187 (1991)(striking down ban a on hiring fertile women for fetal-protection reasons); *Johnson v. Transportation Agency*, 480 U.S. 616, 647 (1987)(Justice O'Connor concurring)(upholding sex-based employer affirmative action program); *Bazemore v. Friday*, 478 U.S. 385 (1986)(rejecting race-based wage disparities); *Meritor Savings Bank v. Vinson*, 477 U.S. 57 (1986)(prohibiting sexual harassment); *Hishon v. King & Spalding*, 467 U.S. 69 (1984)(banning sex-based denials of promotions in law firms); *Arizona Governing Commission*

v. Norris, 463 U.S. 1073 (1983)(invalidating sex-based pension payments).

A historical reality that supports Congress's §5 power to reach private-sector employment discrimination is that many states enacted laws during the twentieth century requiring employers—both public and private—to discriminate against women workers, and these laws had far-reaching effects in causing, reinforcing, and institutionalizing gender discrimination in both spheres. Since Congress could clearly use its §5 authority to ban such state laws, it seems likely the Court would rule Congress could use the same authority to reach the effects that this explicit state action caused in the private sphere. For more information about the state laws on the books when Title VII was enacted, see Barbara Allen Babcock, Ann E. Freedman, Eleanor Holmes Norton, and Susan [Deller] Ross, *Sex Discrimination and the Law: Causes and Remedies* 261 (1975) (describing state laws still on the books in 1968, four years after Title VII was enacted, including those of thirty-nine states that limited women's working hours, thus cutting women off from a multitude of lucrative jobs paying substantial overtime; twenty-six states that prohibited women from working in mining, bartending, or other occupations; nineteen states that prohibited or regulated women's night work; eleven states that set limits on the amount of weight women workers could lift, again barring them from lucrative jobs; and seven states that prohibited women from working before or after childbirth). See generally, *id.* at 246–82, and at 19–53, for the history and long-term effects of this legislation, e.g., the institutionalization of profound sex segregation in the job market.

Of course, whatever the constitutionally permissible source of its power, Congress was acting to eradicate pervasive discrimination and to uphold human dignity when it enacted Title VII.

47. See, e.g., Kingsley R. Browne, "Title VII As Censorship: Hostile-Environment Harassment and the First Amendment," 52 Ohio St.L.J. 481 (1991); Eugene Volokh, "Freedom of Speech and Workplace Harassment," 39 UCLA L. Rev. 1791 (1992).

48. *Pittsburgh Press Co. v. Pittsburgh Commission on Human Relations*, 413 U.S. 376, 389 (1973).

49. *Hishon v. King & Spalding*, 467 U.S. 69, 78 (1984)(quoting *Norwood v. Harrison*, 413 U.S. 455, 470 [1973]).

50. *New York State Club Association, Inc. v. City of New York*, 487 U.S. 1 (1988); *Board of Directors v. Rotary Club*, 481 U.S. 537 (1987); *Roberts v. United States Jaycees*, 468 U.S. 609 (1984).

51. 468 U.S. at 623.

52. *R.A.V. v. City of St. Paul*, 112 S. Ct. 2538, 2546 (1992).

53. *Id.* A year later, in *Wisconsin v. Mitchell*, 113 S. Ct. 2194, 2200 (1993), Justice Rehnquist's decision for the Court, this time *upholding* a law giving enhanced penalties for race-based hate crimes against a First Amendment challenge, pointedly noted Title VII's constitutionality. "Mitchell argues that the Wisconsin penalty-enhancement statute is invalid because it punishes the defendant's discriminatory motive, or reason, for acting. But motive plays the same role under the Wisconsin statute as it does under federal and state antidiscrimination laws, which we have previously upheld against constitutional challenge. *See* Roberts v. Jaycees, 468 U.S., at 628; Hishon v. King & Spalding, 467 U.S. 69, 78 (1984).... Title VII, for example, makes it unlawful for an employer to discriminate against an employee '*because of* such individual's race, color, religion, sex, or national origin.' ... In Hishon, we rejected the argument that Title VII infringed employers' First Amendment rights. And more recently, in R.A.V. v. St. Paul, 112 S. Ct. at 2546, we cited Title VII ... as an example of a permissible content-neutral regulation of conduct."

54. The conference where an earlier version of this article was first presented was held on October 16, 1993, just one week after the argument to the Court in *Harris*, and three weeks before the Court's November 9 decision. The author predicted that the Court would reach "the same result in *Harris*" as it had in the other cases upholding women's equality rights against First Amendment challenges, noting that "at the argument last Wednesday, not one member of the Court asked a single question about the First Amendment."

55. 114 S. Ct. at 370 (quoting *Meritor Savings Bank v. Vinson*, 477 U.S. 57, 64 [1986], some internal quotation marks omitted).

56. *Id.*

57. *Id.* at 372. Following in the footsteps of Justice O'Connor, Justice Ginsburg used the occasion of her first opinion in a women's rights case to suggest that "it remains an open question whether 'classifications based upon gender are inherently suspect.' See Mississippi Univ. for Women v. Hogan, 458 U.S. 718, 724, and n.9 (1982)." (Quoting Justice O'Connor) *Harris v. Forklift Systems, Inc.,* 114 S. Ct. 367, 373, n.1 (1993)(Justice Ginsburg, concurring opinion).

58. 114 S. Ct. at 370.

59. This issue was not fully litigated because Teresa Harris's lawyers unfortunately conceded it in her final brief: "The parties agree that unwelcome workplace conduct should be considered from the viewpoint of a reasonable person in the position of the plaintiff." Reply Brief of Petitioner at 9, n.4, *Harris* (No. 92–1168). This concession dramatically undermined the efforts of many amici to point out the dangers of using a reasonableness standard at all. See Brief of the Women's Legal Defense Fund et al. at 21, *Harris* (No. 92–1168)("Application of 'Reasonableness' Standards for Determining the Severity or Pervasiveness of Harassing Conduct Has Legitimated Discriminatory Conduct and Reinforced Stereotypes"); *id.* at 21–29; Brief of Amici Curiae NOW Legal Defense and Education Fund, Catherine A. MacKinnon, et al., in Support of Petitioner at 21–22, *Harris* (No. 92–1168)("Reasonableness, whether couched in the language of a reasonable person or a reasonable women, operates as a vehicle for the introduction of sex stereotyping, diverts the otherwise straightforward Title VII inquiry into the defendant's conduct, and devolves into an inquiry about the character of the victim in light of societal norms."); *id.* at 15–22; Brief Amici Curiae of the NAACP Legal Defense and Education Fund, Inc., and The National Council of Jewish Women in Support of Petitioner at 21–22, *Harris* (No. 92–1168)("The day is long past when this Court would entertain any suggestion that some forms of racial abuse are legal because 'reasonable' blacks would not be offended"; "the right to equal treatment . . . does not ebb and flow with popular or judicial notions of what forms of discrimination a 'reasonable' black would find tolerable or 'merely annoying' "; *no* woman should have to endure "derogatory or unwel-

come sexual remarks" as a "condition of her job."); *id.* at 21–24. If courts continue to excuse, as unobjectionable to "reasonable people," truly outrageous workplace conduct—e.g., the Sixth Circuit's allowing men to call women "whores," "cunt," "pussy," and "tits"— litigators will surely revisit this issue.

60. On remand, the trial court awarded Teresa Harris $151,435 in damages, interest on that amount, attorneys' fees and costs, and an injunction requiring Forklift to stop engaging in "conduct of a hostile nature toward women" and to adopt a sexual harassment policy. *Harris v. Forklift Systems, Inc.*, 66 Fair Empl. Prac. Cas. (BNA) 1886 (M.D. Tenn. 1994).

61. See *Collin v. Smith*, 578 F.2d 1197 (7th Cir.), *cert. denied*, 439 U.S. 916 (1978).

62. Kingsley Browne, "Title VII As Censorship: Hostile-Environment Harassment and the First Amendment," 52 Ohio St. L. J. 481 (1991).

63. 760 F. Supp. 1486 (M.D. Fla. 1991).

64. 760 F. Supp. at 1493.

65. *Id.*

66. See 760 F. Supp. at 1496.

67. *Pickering v. Board of Education*, 391 U.S. 563 (1968).

68. 274 U.S. 357, 377 (1927).

69. 760 F. Supp. at 1494.

70. *Pruneyard Shopping Center v. Robins*, 447 U.S. 74, 81 (1980); but see *New Jersey Coalition Against the War v. J.M.B. Realty Corp.*, 138 N.J. 326 (1994), finding that shopping malls must permit leafletting under the New Jersey Constitution.

71. 422 U.S. 405, 417 (1975).

72. *United States v. Paradise*, 480 U.S. 149 (1987).

73. *Rabidue v. Osceola Refining Co.*, 805 F. 2d 611, 621 (6th Cir. 1986), *cert denied*, 481 U.S. 1041 (1987).

74. 760 F. Supp. at 1525.

75. Brief Amici Curiae of Feminist Anti-Censorship Taskforce, et al., *American Booksellers Association, Inc. v. Hudnut*, 771 F.2d 323 (7th Cir. 1985) (No. 84–3147), *reh'g and reh'g en banc denied*, 771 F.2d 323 (7th Cir. 1985), *aff'd without op.*, 475 U.S. 1001 (1986).

76. *NLRB v. Gissel Packing Co., Inc.*, 395 U.S. 575, 617 (1969).

77. *Hall v. Gus Construction Co., Inc.*, 842 F.2d 1010, 1012 (8th Cir. 1988). Other names the men called the women included "fucking flag girls," "herpes," and "blond bitch." The men asked whether the women "wanted to fuck" and requested oral sex. Physical gestures included "rub[bing] their hands down the woman's thighs" and grabbing one woman's breasts. Men "frequently pulled down their pants and 'mooned' the women" and "flashed obscene pictures of naked couples engaged in oral intercourse at the women." Gender-based but nonsexual harassment included urinating in one woman's water bottle and in the gas tank of another woman's car, as well as watching the women relieve themselves in a ditch after denying them the use of a truck to go elsewhere for a bathroom break. *Id.*

Contributors

CATHERINE ALBISA recently left her position with the Center for Reproductive Law and Policy and is an attorney in private practice.

DAVID COLE is Professor of Law at Georgetown University Law Center, a volunteer staff attorney for the Center for Constitutional Rights, and a columnist for *Legal Times*.

NORMAN DORSEN is Stokes Professor of Law at New York University School of Law and codirector of its Arthur Garfield Hays Civil Liberties Program. From 1976 to 1991 he was President of the American Civil Liberties Union.

DEBORAH ELLIS is Legal Director of the NOW Legal Defense and Education Fund.

IRA GLASSER is Executive Director of the American Civil Liberties Union.

WENDY KAMINER, a writer, is a public policy fellow at Radcliffe College and the author of four books on civil liberties and social policy issues, including, most recently, *It's All the Rage: Crime and Culture*.

RANDALL KENNEDY is Professor of Law at Harvard University School of Law.

GARA LAMARCHE is Associate Director of Human Rights Watch and Director of its Free Expression Project.

SYLVIA LAW is Professor of Law at New York University School of Law and codirector of its Arthur Garfield Hays Civil Liberties Program.

MARTIN REDISH is Professor of Law at Northwestern University School of Law.

SUSAN DELLER ROSS is Professor of Law at Georgetown University Law Center and director of its Sex Discrimination Clinic.

www.ingramcontent.com/pod-product-compliance
Lightning Source LLC
Chambersburg PA
CBHW022015290426
44109CB00015B/1172